How To Be The Man Women Want: The Get More Confidence and Meet Better Women Guide To Dating

Also by Romy Miller:

Understanding Women: The Definitive Guide to Meeting, Dating and Dumping, if Necessary

Man Magnet: How to be the Best Woman So You Can Get the Best Man

How to Be Wanted: Use the Law of Attraction to Date the Man You Most Desire and Live the Life You Deserve

How To Be The Man Women Want: The Get More Confidence and Meet Better Women Guide To Dating

By

Romy Miller

The Book Factory

Disclaimer: This book is not intended to replace medical advice or be a substitute for a psychologist. The author and publisher expressly disclaim responsibility for any adverse affects of this book. Neither author nor publisher is liable for information contained herein.

How To Be The Man Women Want: The Get More Confidence and Meet Better Women Guide To Dating
by
Romy Miller

The Book Factory
an imprint of New Tradition Books
ISBN 1932420851

For information contact:
The Book Factory
newtraditionbooks@yahoo.com

For the men women want.

Contents

What this book is and what this book isn't.

This book is about becoming the best you can be. And it doesn't take much. What it does take is a willingness to look inside yourself and motivation to change. Change happens best when it comes from within. If you are ready to figure out why you aren't dating as much or as well as you'd like to, you've come to the right place.

This book is mainly about helping you overcome hindrances. We will look into issues of self-esteem, heartbreak and other things that might be holding you back. If you are willing to do the work required, you can and will overcome the obstacles that might be keeping you from being all you can be. This means you can become the man women want. And, after that, dating is easy. In fact, it will become like second-nature. If you can overcome some of your issues, you can rule your own dating life.

On the other hand, this book *isn't* about playing mind games with women. It's not about putting some spell on them to get them to sleep with you. It's not about playing tricks, using worthless pickup lines or mind control. This book isn't about making a fool out of yourself so a woman might pay attention to you.

It's about getting real.

This book is about looking at dating and, perhaps, yourself from a different viewpoint. It's about being willing to see dating in a different light. It's about being willing to see yourself in a different light. If, for some reason, you think you are a loser in love, you can definitely turn that around. And it all starts with you. If you can accept that you might be self-sabotaging yourself, you might be able to stop. This book will help show you how.

Keep in mind that what holds most people back from dating well is themselves. They get notions in their minds about what they can and cannot do. They have many self-imposed restrictions. This book tells you how to overcome these restrictions and get the dating life you want. Because once you can overcome your restrictions, you can actually start doing what you most want—dating well. One way to do that is to give yourself the respect you deserve. If you can start to respect yourself, then you can bet others will respect you, as well.

And isn't it time? Isn't it time to step up to the plate and take a swing? Isn't it time to start looking at dating from a different perspective? Wouldn't you like to view it as something to look forward to and to get excited about? That's the point of this book. It's about putting you in a different mindset. Some men almost break out into hives at the thought of approaching a woman. They don't have that needed confidence to follow through. And so, they retreat. This book is about teaching you how to have that confidence you need in order to approach and date women so retreat is the furthest thing from your mind. In fact, retreat will start to seem silly to you.

This book is about taking the fear out of dating. It's about learning that women aren't *that* unapproachable. Maybe it's just your approach that hasn't been working. If you knew how to do it better and how to get better results, wouldn't you do it? Sure, you would. And I hope to teach you how.

You need to know that this book, just like any book out there, isn't offering you instant gratification. It's mostly a wake-up call. *It's about getting real.* I am going to tell you how you can become the best you can be so you can get the best out of life. If you are willing and able to do so, come along for the ride. If this is something you really want, then all you need to know is that it is possible. It doesn't take much. But what it does take is a willingness to see things differently. And, mostly, it takes a willingness to see yourself differently. Once you can do that, you can become the man women want. You can be one of those guys that women love and desire.

And isn't that what you really and truly want? If so, read on.

On becoming the man women want.

There are a lot of men out there who have no trouble whatsoever attracting women. They have what women want. They know how to talk to women, how to ask them on dates and they know how to actually *date* them so both parties get something out of the relationship. These men know women because they *like* women and they want to get to know them better.

Who are these men?

These are guys you probably know or know of. They are the guys in the clubs and at the parties that women flock to. They know how to make them smile, turn them on and get them interested. They are the men women want.

Why isn't this you?

Yeah, why not you? Why aren't you one of these guys? What is the difference between you and them? When you get right down to it, there's not much difference at all. The difference lies in the perspective. These guys are perceived differently from other guys. Therefore, they act differently and are received differently. They can do so much more than most guys and get away with a lot more, too. In fact, these guys are never lacking for a date and certainly never worry about getting a phone number. It doesn't even cross their minds to be uncomfortable about asking for a number. They aren't just playing the game of love; they are playing it well

They know it. The women they pursue know it. And everyone's happy.

Why?

Okay, look at one of these guys. Sure, he's pretty cute, but not movie star handsome. There's a certain boyish quality to him, or maybe even a manly quality to him that women dig. And all men have either one of these qualities. They're either boyishly charming or have a masculine attractiveness. Both of these qualities women adore. And you have one or the other, even if you don't recognize it.

Right now, figure out which one you have. And once you do, *own it.* You're either the boyish guy women adore or the masculine guy they love. Either quality is one worth having, so if you're boyish, don't worry about the masculine and vice versa. You are who you are, so own it right now. Embrace it.

Now, take another look at these guys. What are they doing that's so right? Why do women dig them so much when they don't even bat an eye at most other guys? What do they have that sets them apart? Are they super rich? Usually not. Do they drive big, fancy cars? Sometimes, but not always. Are they talented in some way the rest of you aren't? Nope. So what is it? Why them and not you? Well, why *not* them? I mean, why *can't* they do this? Why not?

Do you get it? Why *not* them? Why *can't* they be the men women want? Why not? Nobody ever told them *not* to be the man women want. But, most importantly, they never let anything stand in their way of attracting women. They don't let their lack of confidence or low self-esteem or any other issue they have get in their way of getting what they want.

So, now the question becomes: Why can't you be this guy?

Let's face it. You want to be that guy, don't you? I know you do. All guys do. All guys want to be that guy women love. The funny thing is, you can be that guy. Even better, it doesn't take much for you to be him. Well, keep in mind that it will take some work and some change in your attitude, but once you get these things taken care of, you will be the man women want.

And that's what this book is all about. It's about knowing that you can date whatever woman you want, within reason, of course. It's not going to be easy but that doesn't mean you have to make it hard. If you are willing to tweak yourself a little, if you are willing to be open to new ideas and if you are willing to listen to what I have to say, you can become the man women want.

But first, you have to commit. You also have to admit that it's time you make a change. If you already view yourself as perfect, then you don't need this book or any other advice anyone could give you. If you think you are prefect the way you are, then congratulations. You are one in a million.

But, on the other hand, if you are guy who really wants to get out of a dating slump, or even just to start dating in the first place, this book will help you get your dating life up off the ground.

This isn't about playing games. It's about getting out there and finding the woman—or women—you want to date. This isn't about putting out a false image of yourself hoping someone will latch on and love you for. It's about getting real and being honest and moving forward. It's about getting you ready—mentally and physically ready—to get out there and get the dating life you want. If you are stuck in a dating rut, hopefully you can overcome it by the end of this book. However, it is up to you to take the initiative to help yourself. All I can do is supply you with the tools.

Keep in mind that this book will be one hard truth after the other. And, as we all know, the truth hurts. However, the truth can and will set you free. The truth can help you overcome so many obstacles you might begin to wonder why you had issues to begin with. Nevertheless, if you're not ready to take on these challenges, then this book might not be the one for you. I am going to tell you how to be the man women want and I won't hold any punches in order to do so. In the end, I hope I will dispel some myths and, perhaps, some of your frustrations about the whole thing.

And that's all I'm going to say on that.

The most important thing I hope you will get from this book is that there is nothing wrong with you. You are not imperfect. You don't have to mold yourself into a different person in order to attract women. Sure, you do have to tweak and come to terms with some things, but it's not about changing your personality. It's about using what God gave you to land some hot babes.

You are not an unlovable person because you don't go out on many—or any—dates. What's wrong is probably the way you approach dating. If you can begin to approach it more realistically and a little less seriously, then you can become the man women want and, sometimes, women chase after.

Is that what you're after?

If you listen to my advice, there will soon be no stopping you. Once you get over looking at dating as a hassle and start looking at it as something fun to do in order to get to know others, you will begin to wonder why you thought it was a bother in the first place.

Like I said before, this book isn't going to offer you instant gratification. It is, however, offering you a wake-up call. I won't tell you how to play games or give you advice that doesn't work. I am just, simply, going to tell you know it's done. What you do with it then is up to you. You deserve the best, don't you? In order to get it, you just have to face some realities. And once that's done, you can get to the fun part—knowing what it's like to be the man women want.

Are you ready?

In order to become the man women want, you must be ready. You must be ready to make changes and you must be ready to overcome your hindrances to these changes. This means getting over your heartbreak and resistance to change, which we will discuss later. This means setting aside any grievances and resentments you may have built up over time. This means getting over your hang-ups.

So, are you hung-up? Think about that. Having any sort of hang-up is like telling yourself you're going to be stuck forever. Having a hang-up on any issue in regards to dating is like putting a vibe out there that tells women you're a guy with issues. And that's one thing you don't want to be. Everyone has their own issues to contend with so most women don't want to get involved with a guy whose issues might eclipse her own.

It's not that difficult to overcome issues. All you have to do is first recognize that you *have* issues, or hang-ups, or whatever you want to call them. Once you do that, once you admit you have something going on that might be blocking you from happiness and a better dating life, you can see through the problem and to the solution. And once you do that, all you have to do in order to get over it is *release*. And all releasing entails is letting go.

Now the problem with releasing is that most people don't know how. One way to look at it is to think about something you really want but isn't happening. It could be to date a gorgeous woman, get a sports car or whatever. Take your pick. Now when this thing you want isn't within reach, it causes frustration, anger and a fair amount of anxiety. This isn't a good combination. If you are storing up this negative energy, any woman you come in contact with will pick up on it and probably not want anything to do with you.

However, if you take your desire and you release on it, it's got a much better chance of happening. But if you try to control the outcome of it, it's never going to be what you want. In a way, it's like you're saying, "I have to have this or that by this date and if it doesn't happen in precisely the way I want, I don't want it." This is a very constricted way of viewing things and full of control. This might just be the real reason you're not accomplishing your goals. When you try to control the situation, what you most want suddenly becomes an impossible goal to attain. If you are feeling like this, you might not be ready to become the man woman want.

And you have to be ready. You have to be willing to release all your preconceived notions of what you think women want in a man and what you think you have to offer them. You have to get over any hang-ups you might have regarding whatever issue it is that you're mired down in.

All you have to do to overcome all this is to release. This doesn't mean to give up on what you want. It means to give up on the outcome of your desires. Sure, you might want a woman who is built like a fifties movie star, but what if a cute, flower-power chick enters your life and wants you? If you're hung up on the movie star, you won't see the flower chick and might miss out on a great love experience.

But if you release, then you will recognize when a great love enters your life and you will be willing to go for it. That's all it means to release. Release simply means getting out of your own way of happiness. It means to let go o control. Being ready to do this means *letting go* of control. It means giving yourself over to the process of finding good, true love. It means opening yourself up to the possibilities that might enter your life. And, most importantly, it means being open enough to recognize the possibilities that come along. It also means getting out of the way of your life and your success.

And all you have to do is release. Release the outcome and your preconceived notions. First of all, figure out what you want. Is it a long-term relationship? Is it a fling with an older woman? Is it just to go out and be comfortable in clubs and have a good time? Figure out exactly what you want and then... Forget about it. Let it percolate. And then the inspiration of how to do it will come to you. (You can use this with any aspect of your life, too, in regards to careers, housing or whatever.)

Of course, you might be afraid to release. A lot of people are. They think if they don't have total control over something, something bad might happen or something might go wrong or they might not get what they want. But they never realize none of us have total control. *We don't have total control!* Once you accept this truth, it might just open you up to the real possibilities of life.

When you find yourself in this sort of situation, you are letting fear guide you. Whenever you are afraid to let control go, that's just fear. This might be why you aren't dating as much—or as well—as you'd like to. If you try to control every single thing that happens, then you're not living in the moment and probably setting yourself up for a lifetime of disappointment. And you are *resisting* what you have and, thus, blocking what you want.

Resistance comes about because of fear. If you find yourself resisting anything in your life—from your job, car, apartment or the women you tend to meet—then you are basically saying, "I don't want this and until I get what I want, I won't have anything." And you find yourself in a miserable situation. Carl Jung said, "What we resist, persists." Think about that. If you are in a constant stare of resistance, have you noticed that everything tends to stay the same? Soon enough, you whole life is comprised of things you "don't want." When this happens, the resistance keeps building up. Once this happens, something has to change, right? And all you have to do is start releasing. That's it! Once you release, you will be ready to get out there and find the woman of your dreams. Until then, though, you're probably going to be a miserable person.

It doesn't have to be like that. If you want to be the man women want, let go of some of the control. Throw the reins aside and step down. You might be thinking, "That sounds great, but if I let go, she might just slip right out of my life." Again, the fear! So what if "she" takes a hike? Can't there be more than one "she?" Yes, there can be and there is! There are lots of women in the world, man! And most of them want a good man. Just because things didn't work out with her, doesn't mean another won't pop up in her place. This is called having faith. Just because the one thing you really, really want doesn't happen doesn't mean another good thing *won't* happen. And when you let go of control, you might just see that it does.

What do you have to lose? Nothing but waiting on some chick or whatever to materialize. Stop waiting and start enjoying! You have to be ready for this and being ready means letting go of control and just going with the flow.

So, figure out what you want. Release it. And live your life. Keep on truckin'! Don't hold out until something big comes along; take the small accomplishments and enjoy them.

And now, ask yourself: Am I ready? Am I ready to release all the hogwash that's been building up in my mind? Am I ready to move forward and find some good love? And, am I willing to do what's necessary in order to accomplish my goals?

If you answered yes, then you're ready. And that's the first step you need to take in order to get on with your life and live a happier existence.

Hope.

You've probably heard that saying, "Hope is the mother of all fools." I know I have. It's a saying that is loaded with desperation and disenchantment. Two things you don't want to find yourself in the throes of. But what if you've given up hope of ever meeting someone? Is that you? If so, it's time to get up off your butt and decide, once and for all, what you want out of life and out of a relationship.

I know it's hard, though. I know it's hard to keep trying only to get shot down. I know it's hard to even fantasize about meeting someone special. I know it can be difficult to go into a club or bar and look around and see yet another disheartening evening. And going in with that attitude, without much hope, can be a real downer. The trick is to ignite your hope once again and to go into these situations with renewed vigor.

So, ask yourself: What do I hope for? Can I do this? Do even want to do this? Sure, it's hard to put yourself out there because of fear of getting shot down, but isn't it easier than being alone every single night of the week? Think about it. Which do you prefer? An evening which might be tinged with hope, with the possibility of meeting some hot babe? Or an evening of sitting home watching some dumb movie or playing video games?

It's your choice, you know?

How about this? How about instead of feeling dread about going out and meeting someone, you just don't have any expectations? How about just letting go of all that garbage stored inside of your brain from previous bad experiences and getting out there and just being seen? Sometimes just being seen is all it takes for some girl to zone in on you and pick you out of the crowd, especially if you're not trying too hard. She might just want to know what's up with you. Doesn't that give you hope? Good. Because that's what you need.

You need hope in order to proceed. If you have overcome your frustrations, you can see the silver lining in that dark cloud that may have just settled around your head. So, see through the dark and into the light. Feel yourself getting over the hopelessness of it all and see yourself going out there and having some fun.

Once you start to turn it around, you will start to see the possibilities that await you. And once you do that, you can become unstoppable.

The game has changed.

Women aren't like they used to be, are they? Nope. They've changed. So what? Men have changed too. In fact, the world as we know it has changed. But it's not all bad, is it? What's bad is that while everything and everyone has changed, the rules of dating, the game in and of itself, hasn't changed much at all. Sure, it's been reworked and retooled, but mostly this is to no one's advantage.

The game of dating over the last few years has pretty much been skewered. Men and women alike are playing by a different set of rules than even their parents played by. Now we go to bars and clubs and speed dating and internet dating sites to find our new loves. Before, you'd just meet someone through a family member, in school or wherever. You'd meet, there would be an instant attraction and—bam!—you'd fall in love.

Or so the stories go.

Everything always seemed so much simpler back in the good old days. Of course, there were limited choices, too. It was a rarity that anyone would meet and marry someone from another country or whatever. So, while the dating game has changed, if you start to view it in a different light, you just might find it might have changed to your advantage. For starters, women can date and marry the men of their choosing without having to worry about what background he's from or what their parents might think or whatever. They're not so fixated on getting the perfect man either. This means more freedom of choice. This means lots more hot babes to choose from.

See, it's not all bad news. Yes, the game has changed, but it still is focused on the same result—people getting together to have relationships. This is what the bottom line is.

So, in order to get over the newfound game of dating, one must first adhere to the new rules. And by this I mean, get over your hang-ups about dating through internet sites or speed dating or whatever. Open your eyes and your mind will follow. Soon, it will become like second nature.

The game of dating doesn't have to be difficult. It is what it is. And that's all it is. The problem is the frustration you might feel about it. And I know it can be frustrating. However, if you can overcome that frustration and get past your hang-ups, you can go on to enjoy a wealth of possibilities. It means that if you hand yourself over to the process instead of resisting it, you might just find that someone special you're looking for. And that's what it's all about.

Keep in mind that it doesn't have to be difficult. So don't make it difficult! Take the dating game for what it is, get up off your butt and get moving. Time is wasting, so don't waste yours. There are a lot of women out there just waiting for you.

Hot babe magnet.

There are a lot of men out there who are hot babe magnets. They are the very beings that women want. Women crave these guys. They fall all over them. They can't get enough of them. And that's what you want to become. You want to become a hot babe magnet.

So what *is* a hot babe magnet?

Think Steve McQueen. Think Rhett Butler. Think Don Draper. Think *Shaft*! These men are hot babe magnets. They know how to get women and they aren't afraid to get them. Of course, they're actors, playing fictional characters. But even so, study these guys. Find out what they're all about. One thing they all have in common is this: They like women. And they want women. And women return the favor.

Something else they've got? Confidence. They aren't intimidated by women in the least. They don't get fearful whenever they meet a new woman. *They only think of the possibilities.* So the secret of being a hot babe magnet is this: Don't be afraid to go after the woman you want.

Another good way to describe a hot babe magnet as being a man who always gets the woman he wants. He doesn't care how good looking she is, where she works, or what family she comes from or whatever. This is the woman he wants, and he'll have her. If not now, later.

Of course, this doesn't mean for you to be a stalker. There will probably be some women out there who you can't have. They might be married, uninterested, or whatever. This is just the way it is. The key is to not get hung up on one woman. If it doesn't work out, you move on and stop wasting time. A hot babe magnet knows this. He also knows that he's got something great to offer and if a particular woman can't see it, he will find another who can.

On the other side of this, look around at men that you think are hot babe magnets. Notice them in the bars and clubs or wherever. Study them. What do they have that you, perhaps, don't?

The hot babe magnet may or may not be the best looking guy around. He may or may not have the best body, either, or a fat bankroll. He's probably not drop-dead gorgeous. And yet, he's always going out with hot women. In fact, women love this guy. They can't get enough of him. So what does he have that you don't? Is he that special?

Maybe. Maybe not.

The main thing he's got is personality. Well, let me rephrase that. He's got a good personality. He's *comfortable* with himself. And while his personality might not gel with everyone else, he's comfortable with the one he's got and with who he is.

It sounds so simple, doesn't it? But it's true. This guy likes himself and, because of that, women like him. What's great about this is that you already have a personality, just like the rest of us. This means, you already have everything you need in order to become a hot babe magnet. You already have the power within yourself to do this. All you have to do is call it to the forefront and use it to your advantage. All you have to do is wake up and smell the coffee. And you start by admitting that *maybe* you could use a little help in this area. It starts by adjusting your attitude.

Sounds simple, doesn't it? And it is! However, I know some of you will read this and still find fault. You will lament, "But no matter what I do, they still don't seem to want me." Then what you've been doing must be wrong. If you can admit that, you can start to change and with change comes...*possibility*!

This book is about getting on with your life, getting through those self-pitying hurtles that always seem to hold you back. It's about getting out there, finding a good woman—or a few good women—and moving on with your life. If your life is at a standstill right now, it's more than likely due to your attitude. By adjusting your attitude and admitting that you might need a little help and then by accepting the help, you can move forward. And isn't that what you want to do?

Keep in mind, this will entail some effort on your part. Nothing comes that easy. If I could just wave a magic wand and change your life, I would. But I am not a fairy godmother. However, you are grown men and grown men accept responsibility for their lives. It's that simple.

You already have everything you need in order to attract women. What you need to do is bring out the best in yourself so you can have your pick of all the beautiful babes out there.

That's pretty much it, dude. Can you handle it? Or, as you read through this chapter, did you feel slight discomfort? If so, you've got some more work to do. The point of this book is to get you to the point where you *know* you can get a good woman. After you know, then you are ready to go out and find her. And once you're ready to go out and find her, you will have the confidence to follow through.

Settling for less?

Some guys have what I like to call the "low self-esteem" approach to dating. They don't care how a girl treats them as long as she agrees to go out with them. They don't care what they have to do in order to get her attention. They don't really care how much they have to lower themselves in order to keep a relationship.

In effect, they don't much care about themselves. They have the *low self-esteem approach* to dating.

I've seen it a lot, unfortunately. I've seen really good guys get a girlfriend who basically treats them like dirt. She acts like a total bitch and he sits there and allows it. He's just happy someone wants him. He has very low self-esteem.

The only problem with this is this: If you allow anyone to treat you like dirt, they always will. If you never stand up for yourself, people will run all over you. It's that simple. But why would you do this in the first place? Because you have low self-esteem.

Low self-esteem causes so much pain in this world it's unbelievable. At some point, most people are affected by it. However, there comes a time when you have to get over it and start feeling like the good person you are or you will face a lifetime imprisonment of taking other people's crap.

When you have low self-esteem, you not only settle for less, you *expect* to settle for less. It doesn't matter how hard you work to obtain what you have, you think you don't deserve it. Let me ask you this: If you don't deserve what you have, then who does? If you're the one who has worked hard for it, then why does someone else get all the credit?

The main problem when a guy has low self-esteem is this: Women don't like it. You're never going to be the guy women want if you don't think you're good enough to shine their shoes!

Also, having this problem can lead to settling for less of everything in life, including women. If you have low self-esteem, you will inevitably only attract women who will take advantage of you in some way. They're never going to love you for you when you have this problem. They're only going to love you for what you can do for them.

So, if this is you, how do you overcome it? How do you start to feel like a human being who deserves the best out of life? How do you get over your low self-esteem issues? Wow. That's hard, isn't it? And, yet, it isn't that hard. Yes, it's work, but if you're willing to put in the work, you can do. And all you have to do, first, is to recognize that you have this problem. I've always believed the saying that the part of the cure is in the actual diagnosis. And, second, all you have to do is take action to overcome it.

So, recognize that you have low self-esteem and then find ways to overcome it. It might take a few sessions with a therapist. Or it could be as simple as starting to see yourself for the good guy you really are. Instead of putting yourself down for all your shortcomings, look around and take pride in what you've accomplished in life. Know that, deep down, you are a good human being and that you do deserve to be treated like one.

On the other side of low self-esteem are the guys who think they have to put everyone down in the world in order to make themselves feel superior. They might brag about their higher education or sports car or whatever. And while they do this, they make cruel remarks to others who might not be as fortunate. If you are one of these guys, please do yourself a favor and take stock. People do not like people like this. And, keep in mind that most people won't look deeper into the real issue of your low self-esteem to see that what your problem is. They'll simply write you off and not like you very much.

In the end, low self-esteem will only end up biting you in the ass, in one way or another and you'll probably be too depressed or dejected to even know it. Just by taking stock of it and recognizing the problem, you can put yourself on the road to recovery. Keep in mind that it's okay to like yourself and, even better, it's fine to love yourself. Don't get hung up on what you don't have, but focus on what you do. Once you open yourself up to the possibilities, perhaps the door of opportunity will swing open for you. Have some faith.

Waiting for something better.

This is also known as the "I am not settling for less!" syndrome.

Of course, it's not always bad to sit around and wait for someone better to come along, granted that they do, eventually, come along. However, some guys have been waiting for a long, long time. Are you still waiting for someone better?

This type of guy finds fault with every woman he's ever been involved with. She was too fat, or too loud, or she smoked or she had kids or whatever. He just can't commit to her because she's not exactly what he's been looking for. Trouble is, he can't really tell you—or even himself—what he wants out of woman because he doesn't even know.

This guy is in a vicious cycle of love 'em and leave 'em. But right about now, he may be beginning to realize that he needs to get moving before he gets too old. However, if he doesn't wake up and smell the coffee, he will be. That is, if he's lucky enough to get over himself in time.

So, he finds a woman, finds fault and then dumps her. And then he finds another, finds fault and then dumps her. And so on and so forth. What he fails to realize is that the fault does not lie in the women he's dating; it lies within himself.

Heavy, huh? It is.

The problem with having an attitude of, "I have to have the perfect woman or I won't settle," is that you might just end up alone. Women will eventually stop giving a guy like this a chance, especially after he reaches a certain age. When this happens, it's time to reconsider the problem of settling and start asking yourself if it might be you that's the problem and not the women you date.

Sure, everyone wants an ideal mate. They want them to be perfect in every single way. They develop the perfect fantasy of the perfect woman and the perfect life. Nothing is going to stop them from getting what they want. But something always does stop them and that something is reality.

People are not perfect. We all have faults. That's life. It's time to get over it.

Keep in mind that everyone has fantasies and there's nothing wrong with having fantasies. But when fantasies keep you from living real life, they're not fantasies any longer—they're a hindrance to life. If this is you, you really do need to pull yourself together before you become too fixated on the perfect woman. If you do that, keep in mind that soon enough, no ordinary woman will ever measure up to your exacting standards.

If you are still refusing to settle, ask yourself this: *What if my perfect woman never shows up?* And she might not. What if you never meet her? This is a hard reality to face, but by facing it, you are opening yourself up to the possibility of meeting someone pretty darn good. Sure, she might not be perfect, but guess what? You're not either.

You have to realize that this isn't about lowering your standards. It's about opening your eyes to reality and to the possibilities that exist in real life. If you have a fear of settling, then you're missing the point. The point is to find someone you can care about who will, in turn, care about you.

Know that if you try hard enough, you can always find fault in others. You can always find something wrong. We're all human and, as humans, we all have faults. Learning to accept this is the best thing you can do to gain a better relationship. By not looking for fault, you can be more of an accepting, compassionate and caring human being. The kind of guy any woman would be proud to call her boyfriend.

Heartbreakers and the pain they cause.

Your past does not have to dictate your future, but for some of us, this is exactly what happens. You know what I mean, too. Something "bad" might have happened way back when that "scarred" you and now you can't move forward. You may be standing in your own way of moving forward because you're afraid it might happen again. Or, you may think, "Why bother attempting to do something because it didn't work out once before?" You're stuck. You don't know what to do.

It happens to the best of us.

However, in order to be the man women want, you have to get over all this stuff. It's a necessity. Past baggage is what might be standing in your way of getting what you want out of life.

There are several ways to describe this stuck feeling and they are feelings of just plain old disappointment or fear of future disappointment. But, mostly, it can be heartbreak. We've all been there. We've all done that. And, at one point or another, we've all let it trip us up. But we all have to move past it. We all have to get over our heartbreak.

It could have been a girl you lost to someone else. Or maybe she just broke up with you because she was a cold-hearted bitch. Who knows? But this one, this one chick, really did you in. You don't know how you can trust anyone else, right? But, the good news is, you can. And what if they hurt you too? Then that's life, man. Sucks sometimes, doesn't it? But if you never again open your heart to another woman because of one chick somewhere in your past, you will never again experience the true joy of living. And isn't that what you want? Don't you want to feel alive? Don't you want to tingle with excitement when you think about meeting a girl for dinner and a movie?

The other kind of heartbreak can occur from other people in our lives, people we once trusted. It could be a teacher, a former best friend or even a parent. Heartbreak comes in all forms and it doesn't necessarily have to be between a man and a woman.

It's happened to me and it's happened to just about everyone I know. It's called life and that's what happens in life sometimes. And when it happens, we have to reconcile the loss of our dreams, sometimes the loss of love from a friend. This can leave you with bitterness and resentment which, if not taken care of, can build up over time and rot your soul. I hate to put it that way, but I want my point to get made. And the point is that whenever we don't get over our past hurts, we only end up hurting ourselves, ultimately cheating ourselves out of life.

Of course, whenever we experience a loss of this caliber, we don't feel okay within ourselves. We think we have to compensate for the loss and find something that will make us feel better again. Once we can do that, all will be set back in order. Until then, we're not playing.

But it never quite works out like that, does it? All we get back is the feeling of lack that we are putting out. Soon enough, you might think to yourself, "How did my life turn out to be so awful?" And it turned out that way because you let one thing become a life altering event.

Sure, it can be hard not to turn hard and cold once someone betrays us. It's hard to put on a happy face and move forward. But what else can we do? How about if we consider the alternative? And what's that? Get over yourself and get moving with your life.

Yes, I know someone did you wrong and you might want to stay miserable to make them pay. Well, you're going to have to realize that your misery isn't having any effect on their lives, not usually. Usually, they come in, do their damage and go on, probably to damage someone else's life. And by you staying miserable, you're allowing this person to control you. You can't be in a good mood because so-and-so did so-and-so. What bologna! If they treated you crappily and you let it hang you up, either they won't care, will feel good that you're still hung up over them or will think that you're pathetic for not moving on with your life.

Let me put it this way: When you're on your deathbed, do you want to look back over your life and realize that you've had a miserable time of it because so-and-so did such-and-such? If you can overcome this, things can be different. It's hanging on to this misery that keeps you down. But, it's letting go that frees you up to a better life.

You might not realize it, but heartbreak of this kind can taint any future relationship you might have, too. It can lead to repeating the same mistakes over and over. But it doesn't have to! You can get over it and you can move on. And how do you do it? You reconcile it, that's how. Sit down, feel your heartbreak and get over it. Allow whatever feeling you have to emerge, feel them and let them go. And then? You forgive.

Oh, boy, that's hard, isn't it? Forgiveness, which is one of life's great healers, is so hard for many of us to do. We just can't let go of that grudge, can we? We grit our teeth and shake our heads and... End up feeling like crap. That's all it leads to. But if you want to get over it, you have to forgive. You don't have to talk to this person again; you don't even have to tell them you're forgiving them. All you have to do is forgive. And how do you do that? By practice.

If you are ready to make this big step, all you have to do is this: "I forgive_____ for _____." And you fill in the blanks. It might feel a bit uncomfortable at first, so don't force it. Just say it in your mind. Think about what forgiveness means to you. Think about something you might have done to someone else and how you would like them to forgive you. Now take that feeling and apply it to the person you need to forgive. And once you forgive, you can let go. This is what you have to do to move on.

If you never forgive, you can't ever forget. And if you can't ever forget, you have to keep playing the same scenarios in your mind over and over, which, eventually, might drive you mad. But if you learn the art of forgiveness and really mean it when you do it, all that stuff that's been holding you back, making you bitter and giving you frustration will cease to exist.

Not a bad tradeoff, is it?

And, by doing this, you can learn a lot about yourself. You can look at your heartbreak as a learning experience and begin to really understand your boundaries and your sensibilities. You will learn what you will or won't put up with in the future.

By doing this, you will allow newer, better things into your life. But if you hold onto your heartbreak, you're basically asking for an unhappy life. And that's really not a fun way to live, now, is it?

From unwanted to wanted.

It's happened to the best of us, believe me. You love her. She doesn't love you. She loves someone else. Or, maybe, she's just in love with herself. It is the universal problem of unrequited love.

Oh, geez.

When this happens, desire sets into your mind like cheddar cheese on a hot potato. You can't get her out of your mind. She's stuck there. You love her, for God's sake! *You love her.* Soon enough, she becomes an obsession and not in a sexy, perfume ad kind of way, either. She becomes an obsession in the sick-to-the stomach, incessant googling kind of way. But no matter what you do, you can't get her out of your brain. And, so, you begin to feel really badly about yourself.

What's a guy to do?

When you find yourself in love with someone who doesn't love you, it can be one of the most difficult things you can go through. It is emotional hell. There's no other way to describe it. You are, indeed, experiencing unrequited love.

If you find yourself in this position, it will not only make a fool out of you, but it might just keep a lot of good stuff form happening in your life. Essentially, unrequited love blocks real love from entering your life. It holds you back from living life to the fullest. It keeps you from meeting new women. And, mostly, it just makes you plain miserable.

But what can you do? You're in the throes of an unrequited love affair! How do you get yourself out of this mess? Well, the best thing you can do whenever you find yourself in this position is to give up on the girl who's caused it. You have to release her. And then, once you've done that, you can move on. Yes, it will be hard. Yes, there is some pain involved, but once you're over her, you can move on to someone better.

Yes, you can.

One reason people get caught up in unrequited love is because they believe this person is perfect for them. They believe this is the one person in the world who will give them everything they've ever wanted—all the good sex and good feelings that comes from the good love. But unfortunately, this isn't going to happen. Ever. It's done. It's over. Put a fork in it.

One of the best things you can do right now is to recognize what you're doing to yourself. You are putting undue stress on yourself by hanging on when you should have let go. However, if you can let it go and move on, you can go from being unwanted to being wanted.

When you're in this position, you are blocking new women from coming your way. Basically because you're off the market, mentally speaking. And if you're off the market, you can't date anyone else. By getting over her as quickly and as smoothly as possible, you are opening yourself up to newer, better experiences. And once you do that, you can move on. Once you do that, you might just look back and wonder how you got so hung up in the first place. Then you can go from being unwanted to wanted. And usually all it takes is recognizing what you're doing and then stop doing it. Refuse to google her. Refuse to think about her. Wash her out of your hair, man! Get her out of your system. Make a vow to get over her—today—and move on what your life

Let her go her own way and you go yours. And start right now.

Breaking an obsession of any kind is hard, but if you're diligent with it, it can be done. And mostly it just takes refocusing your attention on something constructive. So, refocus and get her out of your hair. And then get ready to move on. There are other women out there just waiting on you to get over her.

So, are you about ready to meet them or not?

It's time to get over yourself.

One way to get on the road to becoming the man women want is to clean your slate. And by this I mean, clear out anything in your past that might be holding you back from becoming the man you are supposed to be.

Imagine a big chalk board and write on that board everything that bothers you. Write down previous mistakes and girlfriends who treated you badly. Write down all your regrets and issues. Write as much or as little as you need to. And then what? Wipe them clean. That's right, clean off all the resentment you might have because of these things. Clean off all the mistakes. Clean off every single thing that is holding you back. Get as close to a perfectly content state as possible.

The things that happened way-back-when don't have to haunt you day in and day out. What's the big deal if your last girl dumped you? It means you weren't compatible and she did you a big favor. *Yes, she did.* Even though it might still hurt and you might still feel that sting of rejection, by her doing this, she has saved you a lot of trouble. She's someone else's problem now. This means there is someone out there who is better for you.

Now, imagine wiping everything off—all those bad dates and blunders and embarrassing moments. All those bad relationships, or hit or miss ones. Wipe off all the chicks that blew you off. Forget about the ones who might have used you. Take away any cringe moments you might have just because at that time, you probably weren't using good judgment for whatever reason.

All these things are in your past and that's where they should remain—a distant memory. You don't have to keep reliving them and making yourself feel bad. You don't have to settle for less or stop trying to date just because of something that happened. It's time to stop punishing yourself. And, seriously, that's pretty much what you're doing when you relive all this stuff. So, stop doing it.

The next step is to erase all you've been taught about women and dating by the media, your friends and, even, your parents. Yes, all these people may have had good intentions, but it might not have been the best advice for you. Just take away whatever advice that wasn't necessarily in your best interest and keep what you need. Clear your mind of the mumbo-jumbo and set yourself free.

Another thing to get rid of is all the romantic movies you might have seen. All the fairy tale stuff that really doesn't mesh with reality. Wipe away any preconceptions about what dating "should" be like and begin to accept it for what it really is—a way to meet someone special. Wipe away the notion of settling for less, or, even, waiting for something better.

Once that's done, wipe away anything others might have told you that put you down. If someone said you were fat or ugly or just plain not good enough, wipe it off. You are starting with a clean slate and you don't need this anymore. Getting rid of this will boost your self-esteem and that's what we're after. So, forget about anyone who made you feel badly about yourself. *Don't let them stop you from moving forward.*

Now that you're done, the best thing you can do is to make your own rules to dating. Yup, that's right. Think about what you want to do and then do it. Make your own rules to getting the woman you want. You and you alone know what's best for you. Make your rules by using the guidelines in this book, but shape them into whatever works best for you. Keep in mind that everyone is different and this means that what works well for some, might not work for others.

Most importantly, know that from now on, you are in control of your own destiny. This means, you have to take the blame away from everyone else and take complete and total responsibility for yourself. Today is the day that you start anew. And you can do that once you clean your slate. This will rid you of all your encumbrances and allow you to start fresh.

And, lastly, if you have any issues dealing with money—bankruptcy, etc.—it's always a good idea to work on that before you bring someone new into your life. Get your finances straight so you can focus on what's really important and that is finding the woman of your dreams.

So, say bye-bye to the old you by cleaning your slate and hello to the new you—becoming the man women want.

Stop worrying about getting laid.

I know one of the main incentives of dating for men is sex. Surprise, surprise. *Shocker!* I understand this is a big deal for you guys. Having said that let me say this: Stop worrying about it so much!

The problem with always having sex on the brain is that when you do, you go into any situation involving the opposite sex with an agenda. Your agenda, obviously, is to get laid. And the problem with this is that it puts you in a one-down position with women. It also reeks of desperation and, even if you think you're not giving off that vibe, women can smell it a mile away.

Desperation isn't a good look for anyone. It's a big turn-off. However, for some, they don't even know when they're being desperate. But if you go into every situation thinking about sex, obsessing about it, then you will come off as being desperate. Your hormones are always in overdrive. You're probably a little jittery and nervous and this will come off as just plain creepy to the women you meet.

The main problem with this is that when you think like this, you risk coming off as being needy and no chick really wants a needy guy. When you come off as *having* to get laid, it makes women cringe. They wonder, "What is up with this guy?" And, "Uh, no, he wants something from me. Best to nip this in the bud right now." And then they get turned off from you.

Essentially, it puts them in a position where they are *expected* to fork over something they may not be ready to fork over. Think of it this way: Have you ever been walking down the street and you see someone who is trying to sell something? If you're not looking to buy anything right then, you will avoid this person. Right? You know whatever they're selling you don't really need or even want. So, you sidestep them and walk on. It's the same principal. If a woman knows that all you want from her is sex, she is going to sidestep you, just as you would the vendor on the street.

Now I know there are a lot of books out there that tell you how to get women into bed. They offer a lot of empty promises and can make you look like a creep, or, at the very least, a fool. Sure, you can use these techniques and maybe even get lucky—possibly one time out of a thousand. But what you're not going to get is any sort of fulfilling relationship. And I know that might not be what you're after. Maybe all you want is to just get laid. If this is your end-all-be-all, then why not ask yourself why. Is it that important? Are you going to die if you don't have sex soon?

Well, let me tell you, if you actually put in the time to get to know a woman in the way I am telling you, you stand a helluva better chance of getting laid than you would using some sort of pick-up method. You could try that for years before it works. This way works more quickly, but you do have to be willing to commit to someone. You have to be willing to respect women as human beings. And if all you want is a quick roll in the hay, you're not giving them any sort of respect. Women know this. That's why they avoid guys who only want sex.

One reason you might be thinking about getting laid so much is because of all the over-sexed teen comedies out nowadays. In these movies, total losers find women who are so pretty and so horny they can't help but get laid. This may have put some false expectations in your mind—*if he can do it, so can I.* Well, hate to tell you, but "he" is a fictitious character and what works for a movie subplot won't ever work in reality. These movies are fun to watch, sure. But just be entertained by them. Don't make them into a life plan.

You have to know that women aren't really looking to get laid all that much. Yes, they do like sex as much as men, but mostly in the confines of a relationship. This is because of the possibility of pregnancy. If she gets knocked up with some guy she just met, well, what's she going to do? She doesn't know this guy. She doesn't know if he even wants—or likes—kids. This puts her in a pretty pickle. If she gets pregnant, she's got a big headache. What's the guy who got her pregnant got? He might end up with a guilty conscience, but he isn't committed to doing anything. He can walk off, scott-free. After all, he's not the one who's pregnant, now, is he?

Can you see my point? If you look at it this way, you might understand why women aren't just jumping into bed with every man they run across. You might understand why pick-up tactics don't usually work. And you might even begin to relax a little and take the pressure of getting laid off of yourself. So what if you don't get laid soon? The world is not going to end.

And this brings us back to my point. If all women think you want is sex, they won't want to get to know you better. They know if they give it up that night, you will probably be gone in the morning. This puts a wall up between you and them. And it will be hard to mount that wall once it goes up.

Sure, sure, I know you probably know some guy who gets laid left and right with no strings attached. He's probably out whooping it up all the time. Big deal. After a while, however, all he will be able to do is have sex. He won't know how to have a real relationship. However, once he hits a certain age, he won't even be able to have sex that much, either. Once he gets older, he won't be as fun as he once was. And one of the main reasons this guy gets laid is that he's probably around a lot of very drunk women. Or, he's around women just like him.

Remember, sex is a very personal experience and many women don't want to give it up just because of that. They only want to give it up to a guy they know isn't being desperate and to a guy who isn't expecting it as some sort of payment for dinner or whatever.

Women like strong men and being strong entails getting your hormones under control. I wish there were a more delicate way to put this, but there isn't. So, when you make overtures at someone in hopes of getting laid, you are at risk as being seen as suspect and partly disingenuous. And that leads to looking needy. No one wants that. Do you? Of course not.

All you have to do to get this situation under control is monitor yourself a bit. This doesn't mean to change your whole personality or demeanor. It just means to put a lid on the whole "I need sex and I need sex now and that is making me feel very needy and desperate" situation. Remember when you're out, you're just out to have a good time, just like anyone else. If it leads to something, then it does. If it doesn't, you won't be crushed or angry about it. This puts you into a whole different category with women. You're the cool guy; you don't care if she gives it up to you or not. This lends itself to mystery and women love mystery. It is a huge aphrodisiac to women.

Once you get this under control, you will have women wondering what is up with you. They will think, "He's very interesting, but somewhat aloof. Yet, he doesn't seem interested in me in that way. What's up with that? Hmmm…"

Do you see how this works? It works by letting them know that while you are interested, you're not so interested that another girl can't come along and turn your head. This sparks interest in them and they will want you all to their selves.

In essence: If you act like your life depends on some chick making it with you, you'll never find one who will. However, if you pull back and act like you can take it or leave it, there might be more than a few takers. All this entails is that you get your mind off getting laid and not putting out that desperate vibe. This means, just go out to go out and have fun. Go out to meet some new people. And don't go out with the sole intention of getting laid.

Remember when…?

Once you begin to get over all your hurdles and start to become the man women want, you will have a good reason to get out there and find those women who are waiting for you. You might even begin to look forward to it, too. Can you remember a time when dating was fun and exciting? It used to be fun and exciting, didn't it? It used to be something that you just did instead of something you felt obligated to do. You weren't stressed about it, were you? You weren't "on the hunt" then so much, were you? It wasn't a dire, life or death situation. It was just a time that you just went out, had some fun and didn't have any expectations. In essence, you were in the flow.

Before you got older, didn't you and your buddies go out and have fun? Didn't girls sometimes join in on the fun? Can't you remember when you kept it light and airy and didn't give a hoot if you hooked up or out—you were just out having a good time, after all. Think about that time when there was no pressure to find "The One." Remember when it was just fun to go out and shoot some pool or have a beer or whatever with the guys. Remember when you didn't have any expectations. Remember when you were just out being yourself and how much more fun you had.

Think about it. I am sure it wasn't that long ago. And think about this again: *Remember when you were just out being yourself and how much more fun you had.* This is the feeling you need to reclaim. That feeling is what is going to make you more attractive to women. You need to be just a guy out and about having a good time and not really looking for anything. You're open. That's the important thing. You are open to new experiences but at the same time, you're not looking for them.

The most important thing I can stress is this: *Just being yourself will attract women like nothing else.* Think about that for a moment. I want it to sink in. Got it? Good. Let's repeat for emphasis: *Just being yourself will attract women like nothing else.* Women will want to get to know you because you look free—problem free, trouble free, carefree, and free to new opportunities. They'll see you out there having fun and want to know what's going on with you. Why? Because they want to have fun, too. They will want to join your party.

If you can learn to accept yourself, others will automatically accept you. No one is out there trying to change you. Well, maybe your mom is, but that's a different subject for a different book. But, seriously, no one wants you to be something you're not. If it's you that's trying to be someone that you're not, then just stop doing it. Stop trying to change yourself and accept yourself for who you are. You were given a distinct personality. That's what you were born with and to try to alter it is a recipe for disaster. You won't go far pretending to be someone you're not. In fact, you won't get anywhere.

It's important to never give someone a false image of what you think they want. Always give them the real you. So what if you're a little shy around new women? Women love shy men! They see them as a challenge. So what if you get a little loud after a few drinks? Lots of people do. And so what if you come across someone who doesn't like you for you? If she doesn't like you for who you are, she never will. Don't morph into what you think she wants just to get her attention. Just be yourself and wait until someone comes along who will like you for the unique human being you are. And don't doubt that it will someday happen, either. I've seen it happen to guys with such low self-esteem, it's a wonder they could even get out of bed in the morning.

Once you can be yourself, then you can become the man women want. Just be yourself, just be the man you are meant to be. If you've heard something about how women only like a certain kind of man, then you've heard wrong. Women like all kinds of men, but they especially like those who like and accept themselves for who they are. Don't adjust yourself in order to meet someone's criteria. Just allow things to happen naturally. Do not ever try to be this or that because you think it might work better. It never does.

Just be yourself. That's all anyone expects anyway.

Don't be afraid to look her in the eye.

It's all in the way you act, really. It's about treating a woman like she is a woman. Women like to be treated nicely by men, but they don't want a man to act like a wimp or a pushover. They want someone who is willing to go out on a limb and address them. They want a man who acts like a man. So, be the man and approach that woman. And treat her nice. Give her the respect she deserves. And, most importantly, look her in the eye.

Making eye contact is crucial. This lets her know you're not shifty or hiding something. It also lets her know you're comfortable enough with yourself to do that. It lets her know you are, indeed, a man.

If you have trouble with this, it is more than likely due to a self confidence issue, which we will discuss later. I think one good way to figure out if you do have issues with confidence is the degree to which you look people in the eye. If you look around and find that you can't make eye contact, you might have low self-esteem.

And that's not so good; especially if you want to date. Women like men who are confident. Just as men like women who are confident. They want a man who can look them in the eye and be certain of himself.

Let me put it this way: If you can't look her in the eye in the first place, what chance do you have when she wants to pull you into conversation? Not much. Showing her that you're unafraid of how she's going to react to you—by looking her in the eye—lets her know you're a guy who knows what he wants and is willing to take the chance.

So, ask yourself this: Am I willing to take the chance?

Keep it light.

If there's one thing most women hate is a guy with no sense of humor. Sure, she might be an art chick who goes for the brooding guy with the dark side at first, but he's going to wear thin after a while. Most women, generally speaking, like to laugh and they love men who can make them laugh.

Dating can be so serious but it doesn't have to be. If you learn to keep it light and airy, then you can attract more women. One way you do this is by taking yourself less seriously. Also, by taking the seriousness out of dating, i.e. the desperation, you can open yourself up to a whole new group of women who just want to have some fun.

Just by relaxing and acting cool as a cucumber, you can keep it light. By not taking everything so seriously, you can attract women who will want to know you better mostly because you're so easy to be with. If you can be comfortable with yourself you will automatically make her more comfortable with you. And that's what you're after.

The aggressive man.

Women know that men are the pursuers. Women like this fact and use it to their advantage. However, what they don't like is an overly aggressive man, a man who chases and never stops, even when he has been told to. They don't like it when a man becomes obsessed.

You're not this man, are you?

In order to be the man women want, one thing that you can't do is be overly aggressive. Sure, if you see a woman you like and want to give a little chase then go for it. But a little chase simply means being the one who initiates a conversation. It doesn't mean to literally chase her down the street or stalk her.

How can you tell if you're too aggressive? You zero in on a chick and stalk her like prey. Or, if you get her attention, you won't let go of it. You might use forceful body language and stare intensely in her eyes. When you do this, it makes women very uncomfortable and makes them want to bolt.

Sure, sure, we know that most everywhere in the animal kingdom the male has to chase the female. It doesn't take a genius to figure that out. However, while a little chase is great, too much equals a sad, lonely night of television and a TV dinner.

Keep in mind that you will have to put some work into getting a woman. But if you find the perfect one and then hunt her down, you're just going to scare her off. Of course,

I understand you don't want her to get away. She *might* have forgotten to call you. Maybe. However, you can't let your impatience get in the way. If you do this, you end up not only looking like a fool and but also kind of creepy.

If this is you, all you have to do in order to correct this is to monitor your behavior. You should have an outgoing personality without being too aggressive. So what can you do? You do what feels right. Keep in mind that every woman is different and what works with one will not work with another. Always listen to your gut. If you have a feeling you might be making her uncomfortable, then back off. This will save you a lot of trouble and embarrassment. Also, watch her body language. Is she leaning forward or is she leaning back? If she's leaning forward towards you, she's interested. If she's leaning back, not so much. That's an indicator to step away for a while.

Another good way to understand this is to simply put yourself in her shoes. If you are unsure if you're acting inappropriately, then think about how you would feel if someone were doing this to you. By putting yourself in her situation, you will begin to understand the dynamics of your actions. And then you can correct them so you don't come across badly.

Being too aggressive is never good. It can make you look desperate and we've already talked about that. So, just take a chill pill, listen to your gut and then *chill out*. If she gets away, there's more where she came from. But being aggressive will not only scare her away, it will never make you the man women want.

Show just *enough* interest.

Are you interested in getting someone to really like you? If so, one of the main things you can do is to show just *enough* interest. Then you leave them wanting more.

It's not hard to do. Say you meet some hot woman at a party or whatever. You're really, really into her, aren't you? Well, don't show it! Stand around and engage her in conversation for a while, then excuse yourself. Now, don't go back to her for a little bit. Let her watch you, let her get antsy about if and when you're going to come back over. Let her sit for a few minutes. And while you're doing this, if she is interested in you at all, she will wonder what is up with you. This will spark desire because desire comes from wanting something we can't have. If you put yourself into a position of being desirable, all the work is done for you. All you have to do is show up.

Now this does not mean to treat her like dirt or ignore her or whatever. It just means to hold back a little and let her come to you. This leaves her wanting more. It makes her wonder what you're all about. If you can leave a girl wanting more, you can have her.

Many men, for some reason, just don't get this. They think they have to be all over a girl—sometimes any girl will do—and if they keep on her, they'll wear her down and she'll have sex with them. (We discussed the desperation about getting laid earlier.) This is a totally inaccurate way to think. No, you will not wear her down and get into her pants. All you will do is annoy her and ruin her good time.

Now, on the flip side of this, if you meet her, talk with her for a few moments, then disengage yourself, she will think you don't really like her. This will make her wonder why. And it will, in turn, make her want you. Of course, this isn't the case for every single woman out there and every situation you may become involved with. But it will work for most. Use this at your discretion and with women you really like. You don't want to use it on just anyone because if you do, chances are they're going to really like you and if you really don't like them, there will be a big mess to clean up. I'd suggest avoiding this at all costs.

Here are a few tips:
- Never gush or go on about how good she looks.
- Don't ask personal questions.
- Never laugh at a dumb joke—just chuckle.
- And, never, ever show too much interest. Show just enough.

A few words on the last tip, "never, ever show too much interest." If you show someone you're really interested, they will bolt. I've seen it happen time and time again. The odd thing with women is that if you let them in on the fact that you really dig them, they get scared. It's almost like they think you're ready to commit to China patterns and baby strollers. (Yes, some women are as commitment phobic as some of you guys.) This sends up warning signs in her mind and she starts thinking about nightmare scenarios.

Don't ask me why. This is just the way it is. There isn't much logic in the game of love.

On the other hand, if you can learn to hold back, give her some space and not show how much you like her at first, then you've got it in the bag. She's probably going to dig the space and respect you are giving her. This lends itself to trust and with women, trust is a big issue.

You might be wondering how, exactly, you do this. How do you leave them wanting more? Because you have confidence in yourself and you don't come off as desperate and you don't fawn over them, most women you come in contact with are going to want more if you act in this manner. Remember, the chick you've just met is cool—and pretty damn hot—but so what? There are a lot of cool and hot chicks in this world. She's just one, right? This is the attitude you need, even if you do feel butterflies in your stomach. Even if you are so attracted to her you can't stand it. You just need to hold back and reel her in slowly. Never let her know how much you're into her. Soon enough, you will have her hooked and you can reel her in. But take your time in doing so!

This doesn't mean that once you get her phone number you play silly games about calling her. This is about you getting her interest sparked in you. Once that happens, play it like a cool guy, not a douche bag. You don't want to piss her off too early in the game, but neither do you want to crowd her. If you say you're going to call her, then call her. If you ask her out for a date, then show up on time and then take her out and show her a good time.

Keep in mind that this isn't a hard thing to do. Keep a little distance but never be an asshole. Soon enough, she'll be eating out of your hand. Once you've got her hooked, then you can let her in on how you feel. But always leave her wanting more.

How to get them interested in you.

And now for one of the most important lessons in this book. How do you get chicks interested in you? It's easy and kinda funny—you get them interested in you *by acting like you're not interested in them*. To be more specific, you act like you're slightly interested but not *too* much. Yeah, you think she's cute and all that, but you've got things to do. She might be fun to hang around, but so what? Other girls are, too.

If you can master this skill, you can inspire women to want to get to know you. If you can do this, they do most of the work for you. All you have to do is show up, act like a nice guy and keep it cool. This makes them wonder if there is something special about you. Why aren't you falling all over yourself for them? What's so special about you? They won't know and by you holding back, it will make them want to know.

This goes without saying, but I am not saying to act like some jerk who thinks all he has to do is hang back and the women will flock to him. No, you will have to approach women, but you just can't be too eager with them. Yes, you might have to buy a few drinks; you just don't buy them *all* their drinks. You give them a little rope, but never too much that makes them think you're a pushover. Women like a challenge and if you can be seen as a challenge, you can have your pick.

If you're unsure of what I am saying, let me say it again. The more interested you act, the more they will back away.

They might feel like you're smothering them. However, the less interested you act, the more they will want you. It's like they're saying, "Hey, I know I'm pretty hot, so why isn't he into me? Have I done something? Have I not shown enough interest? What is going on here?"

It sounds crazy, doesn't it? Well, it might be crazy, but it's the truth.

Women think that if you're too interested in them you might be a loser. They might look at you as some guy who can't get any chicks, so they don't want to get stuck with you. That's why a lot of women won't talk to you when you approach them. However, by acting not all that interested, you can pretty much bet that they're going to want to know what's up with you. And, soon enough, when you get all the preliminary stuff out of the way, they will know.

The rock star principal.

Women don't really want men to be easy. This is what we discussed in the previous chapter. If you're too gushing or too nice, they end up thinking something is wrong with you. It's like you're on clearance or something. Harsh reality, but true. And if you come on too strong, you end up looking desperate. But what is a guy to do? What can a guy do to let women know he's alive? He can act like a rock star.

Pick your favorite rock star. And if you don't like rock music, just pick your favorite country, opera or whatever star. Think about this guy. What is it about him that's so great? He's rich, of course, and probably somewhat talented. And, most importantly, he's a friggin' rock star! *Hello!*

But, seriously, this guy, this dude, Mr. Rocker, what is so darn special about him anyway? He never has to work for women. He just has them land in his lap. And plenty of them, too. And women, even when they know they might not have a chance with this guy, will do anything to get him. They all want a rock star. *Always.* And they want him because he's pretty much unattainable. Therefore, he's worth fighting for, worth making a fool out of themselves for and worth being turned down by.

He's a rock star. And guess what? You can be one, too.

No, I am not telling you to get the band back together or learn to play the guitar. Unless, of course that's what you want to do. I am telling you that you can take this guy's attitude and use it for yourself. I can hear you say, "But I'm

ROMY MILLER

not cool enough! This guy is cool!" But you can be cool, too
This is about building confidence, which is the mos
important thing you can do. If you can become more
confident, you will become a man women want. Confidence
builds over time, but it is important to start laying the
groundwork now.

Everyone has good qualities. Right? And if you look at
rock stars, you will see that they do too, but they might no
be the best looking guys on earth. But they are confident
They are self-assured and a man who is confident and self
assured will go a long way with women. You are coo
enough to be a rock star even if you can't drink copious
amounts of whiskey. If you think you're not cool enough
you will never be cool enough. Having confidence is nothing
more than telling yourself you're just as good as all these
other dudes. And you are! You can be a rock star with
women!

Never—ever!—underestimate yourself or your worth
That's what gets so many people into trouble and sows the
seeds of self-doubt. You know that you have good qualities
so play on them. If you can afford some new threads, go buy
some. If you can't be a rock star, at least dress like one. Well
maybe not. Some of them dress like they found their clothes
in a garbage can.

The point is, every single person in this world has had
their confidence tested at some point. And some more than
others. It's time to get over it! Claim your confidence and
your right to be a cool rock star guy and then go for it. With
confidence, nothing can stop you. If you think that you are
the best, most everyone else will think you're the best too.

Of course, I am not talking about being arrogant. No
no, no. Arrogance and confidence are two totally different
things. With confidence, you've got the goods to back up the

swagger. With arrogance, you don't and you're hiding behind a façade. And soon enough, the gig will be up.

So, the best way to become the man women want is to get a little confidence. I know it can be a challenge, but it is so worth investing in. Do whatever you have to in order to build confidence and then watch the ladies flock to you. Just as if you were, indeed, a rock star. And, if you don't particularly want to emulate a rock star, just emulate other confident men, whether they are successful business men or cowboys or whatever. It doesn't matter who, just as long as you do.

The importance of first impressions.

"You never get a second chance to make a first impression." How many times have you heard that one? Think about what it means. It means that what you first present to someone upon meeting them is the lasting image they will have in their mind of you, pretty much forever. If you present a cool confidence, that's the way they will think of you. However, if you present an aura of nervousness, then that's they way you will be viewed.

Oddly enough, the importance of first impressions is overlooked time and time again. Even when they're going out of town, some guys still go out of the house looking like they just rolled out of bed. And then they lament about how hard it is to get a date. The thing is, if you don't care how you look, how can you expect anyone else to care? You can't.

But it's not only appearances that are important to making a good first impression. If you meet someone and start off by putting yourself down, even if you are just using self-deprecating humor, they will always look at you in the way you portrayed yourself. For example, if someone compliments you on your hair and you reply, "My hair? It's awful, full of cowlicks. I can't ever do anything with it." Then that person will always view you as the guy with cowlicks. The image you put out of yourself, especially to women, is the image they will always have of you. It is rare that you will come across a person who overlooks this and sees that you're just putting yourself down and then feels sorry for you or whatever. They will really think of you as the guy with cowlicks. This is why it is so important to portray an image of self confidence.

People who are confident within themselves would never put themselves down for any reason in front of another person. And other people rarely think badly of them. In fact, this person with the high self-esteem might evoke some jealously from others because they can see how much they truly like themselves.

You should keep in mind that whenever you first meet people, they aren't looking for fault in you. Most often it is our "bad" self images that we project and this projection is how people will see us. In essence: What we give them is what they get. And if we give them a bad first impression, that's what they'll always have of us.

If you know this might be a problem area for you, then all you have to do in order to stop is to become aware of it. Once you are aware of how you present yourself to others, you can correct this behavior by simply catching yourself when you do it. For instance, if someone gives you a compliment, accept the compliment and respond back with a "Thank you." If you're the kind of person who responds back with a, "Well, yeah, but..." then you are, more than likely, giving off bad first impressions. This also makes you seem not very confident. The reason for this is simple: If you can't take a compliment from someone you know, then it's pretty obvious you won't be able to take one from a complete stranger. What's more obvious is that because you view yourself in a "lesser" way than others, you won't be able to make a good first impression.

When you are trying to become the man women want, a good first impression is key. Without it, there will rarely be a relationship to speak of. It just won't go beyond that awkward introduction. If you find yourself putting yourself down for any reason, stop. I mean it—stop! Stop it right now! Maybe you use this sort of self-deprecating humor as an icebreaker or whatever. No good. Just don't use it at all. If you have to put yourself down in the hopes that others will like you, then those people who would respond well to it aren't the kind any self respecting person would want to find themselves in the company of.

So, once you realize how big first impressions are, you can start to make them. Use this to your advantage. By displaying an image of self confidence, you are not only letting these women know that you like yourself and enjoy your own company, but that they will, too.

Looking for love?

Have you ever lost something and could not, for the life of you, find it? Let's say it was your keys and God knows that this happens to all of us. Where did they go? You search your place from one corner to another, to come up with nothing. And guess what? They are exactly where you left them. *But this is usually only after you've almost given up looking for them.*

Looking for love is kinda like looking for lost keys. The more you try to find love, the harder it is. Have you ever noticed that? The harder you try to meet someone, the more elusive the idea of actually doing it becomes.

You might be thinking, "But if I don't actually look for love, how am I ever gonna find it?" And I would reply, *the answer is in the question.*

Looking for love, just like looking for lost keys, means that you are trying too hard. If you try too hard to find something, it rarely happens. But once you are just about to give up, it happens, almost like magic.

Most people I know tell me that they met their loves when they weren't looking. They were too busy, had too many plans and blah, blah, blah. And then—bam! They found the one they'd always been looking for. It sounds like a romantic comedy or something doesn't it? Well, that's because that's usually how it happens.

It's just that when you look too hard for love, the less likely you will find it. And why is that? It's because you are concentrating on the *looking* and not on the *finding*. This doesn't mean to give up on love. Oh, no, that's not what I'm saying at all. What I am saying is to relax a little bit on it. Chill out some. And let it evolve naturally.

All humans want love. That's all we want. We want to be loved and we want to give our love to others. It's just that sometimes it doesn't evolve quite so naturally as boy meets girl, falls in love, gets married and so on and so forth. Sometimes it's boy meets girl and then gets his heart broken and then get transferred across the country for his job and so on and so forth. Just because love doesn't follow a linear path doesn't mean you should give up on it.

I understand that there is some panic involved in finding love. It's like we want love and we want it now and we think we have to force something into happening. We feel like if we don't try our hardest to do something, it won't ever come about. But if you think about it, it never happens anyway. So why panic? Why hunt love down like a wild animal? Why not sit back and let it happen on its own?

Take internet dating. Everyone's doing it, right. However, if you go into it with any sort of desperation—*must find the woman I want online!*—then you are looking too hard for that perfect match. The idea is that while you're looking, you're not getting hung-up on the ideal. You're just seeing who's out there. You're releasing the outcome.

Remember we talked about releasing? That's all you're doing here. Just release what you want and see it come to you. Stop looking and watch it happen. In an odd way, it's almost like you have to give up on it before it comes knocking on your door. This is, in essence, letting go of control. And once you can learn to do that, you can make anything happen, mostly by just wanting it to happen, but not getting hung up on the where, when and how.

Sometimes, you can be your own worst enemy. You can stand in your own way of happiness without even knowing it. If you are desperate for love and need it, you will, more than likely, turn off any potential dates. This is because you're putting out a vibe of desperation. You might not even be aware you're doing it, either. But once you get desperate, you can block anything from coming into your life. It's like you're putting up a wall between yourself and what you want.

The great thing is that all you have to do in order to turn all this around is to stop being desperate, stop looking for love and start having a positive attitude. Remember, most everything is in your attitude. How you feel about things comes across to those you meet. Sure, having a good, positive attitude may sound kind of hokey, but it's the one thing you can do in order to get the most out of life. If you know what you want and know that you deserve it, getting into a positive mindset is usually all it takes in order to attain it.

Pretty cool concept, huh?

What, exactly, do you want?

In order to become the man women want, you have to know exactly what you want in the first place. If it's a soul mate, then so be it. If it's to date around with a few different women at any given time, so be it.

If you don't know what you want, then how can you ever hope to get it? It seems easy enough, though, doesn't it? Knowing what you want? But many people don't have a clue as to what they want or why they want it. They just know they're lacking something, though they can't put a finger on what it is.

Right now, think about what you want. Seriously. Stop reading for a moment and think about what you want. Be precise. Be specific. And then write it down. Write down every single thing you want. Now look at the list. That shouldn't be too hard to do, should it?

Knowing what you want is paramount in actually *getting* what you want. If you are uncertain about what you want, then how can you ever expect to have your wish granted?

On the other side of this is the important issue of knowing what you *don't* want. Knowing what you don't want is just as important—if not more so—then knowing what you do. So think about this, too. What don't you want? Obviously, a girlfriend who cheats. Maybe not to be stuck in dating hell? Any and all of those things that brings up feeling of negativity is a don't. Write them down, too.

Now that you've figured out what you don't want and what you do, you can actually start to make this stuff happen. Whenever you think about what you want, feel it. See yourself meeting that perfect girl. See yourself on that great date. See yourself being confident and self-assured. See all the things that you want to happen, happen. This is the fun part! Isn't it great to be at this part? So, have fun with it.

This isn't a terribly difficult process, so don't make it one. It should be viewed as like going into your favorite store and buying all the things you want. It's like you're a kid in a candy store again. Be that kid and have fun, even if it's only in your mind right now. Soon enough, it will be in your reality.

So, have fun with it. Make the transition from what you don't want to what you do want. And sit back and watch your life transform.

The lazy boy comfort zone.

It's hard, I know, to get up out of your recliner and do something. It's hard to envision a future of hot chicks. It's hard, I know it's so hard, to turn off the TV, dust the potato chip crumbs off yourself and go into the world and see what you can do. Sometimes it's just so easy to sit back and let life pass you by.

Is this you? Have you found yourself in the lazy boy comfort zone?

Sure, I know you want more out of life. Hell, most of us do. I know you want something better. But, hey, knowing doesn't make it so, brother. You might be looking out the window with some trepidation and a little unease. Life can be better, but what if it never is?

Oh, boy, now I'm depressed, too.

Come on! Get up and get going! Your life is waiting on you! Are you kidding me with this? I think what this is called is feeling sorry for yourself. And, hate to break it to you, but no one wants to be around someone like that.

The day does come when you have to make a choice. You can either sit back and let life pass you by, or you can get up and get to it. The day comes when you have to spread your wings and fly. Sure, everyone wants better, but it's having the cojones to do better for yourself that might be making you a little apprehensive. This feeling of unease comes about because you might just be in a comfort zone. It's a complacent place. It's nice and warm. There's nothing wrong with being comfortable. The problem lies in the fact that comfort zones can take years out of your life. And when you look back and see that all you've done is worked, napped and watched TV, you might get pretty pissed off at yourself.

Is this you? If so, admit it. You don't have to do anything about it, of course, but admitting it is the first step towards curing it. I understand that looking towards the future and envisioning a better life can be a little scary. Hey, it's scary for everyone, not just you. Sometimes it *is* easier just to sit back and let things ride. It can be scary to start looking for a new love. But it doesn't mean you shouldn't do it. It just means you're human. That's all.

Ironically, comfort zones are rarely comfortable. Fear tends to take over when we find ourselves in them. When we're not out trying new things and meeting new people, we begin to think we can't ever do these things. And it gets easier to sit back and let life pass by.

You have to realize that the only way to a better life is to take that first step into the unknown. And this can cause some anxiety. If this is what you're feeling, then you've probably been in the comfort zone way too long. You like what you have now. But don't you want to love what you have? Wouldn't that be so much nicer? But you have to be ready to get that love. Until you're ready, it probably won't happen.

The other problem with comfort zones is that this is where many people get stuck. You get stuck in an okay job and with okay friends and with an okay apartment. Everything is *okay*. It's just *okay*. You might not want to get out of your routine because you just don't want to have to think too much about anything. You've probably worked really hard to get where you are now. You don't want to give it up. But the thing is, you don't have to give anything

up in order to get better. All you have to do is get out o
your comfort zone and be ready for new experiences.

Ask yourself this: While it's all well and good to stay ir
the comfort zone, is this really what you want?

Think about this: Wouldn't it be great to find tha
dream girl? Wouldn't it be nice to go out and be the life o
the party? Or, maybe, even just be invited to a party? Hell
yeah, it would be! It would be so nice! Thinking about stuf
like this should excite you enough to get up and do
something about your situation. If it doesn't, then you are
definitely stuck in the comfort zone and not too far from
giving up. But don't do it! Don't give up! Giving up on life is
for losers and you are not a loser. If you were, you wouldn'
have picked up this book. I know that and you know it. I
you were a loser, you would have already conceded to a
monotonous life. And I'd be willing to bet that you are fa
from doing that.

It's time for you to get excited about your new life. It'
time to overcome any anxiety you might be feeling. It's time
to drop your trepidations and get out there and get going
And you can start right now. All you have to do is feel the
excitement of what's in store for you. Think of all tha
wonderful stuff that is going to happen soon. And once you
do that, not only will your future look brighter, but you
now will, too.

Are you living in reality?

Many people, women included, have preconceived notions of what love, romance and relationships should be about. They have an idea that it's supposed to be *this way* and if it's not *this way*, they can't handle it. If it's not perfect, then there's something wrong.

What you might not understand is that life isn't a romantic comedy, or even a comedy of any sort. Life is just life and it's meant to be lived. What this means is that if you have an idea of the way things are *supposed* to be, you might not be living in reality.

With women, there's the ideal of Mr. Right. All women want this guy. And he's the perfect guy who does everything right and never makes a mistake. If he does make a mistake, then he atones for it and everything goes back to being picture perfect.

Men do this too. They have an ideal Miss Right, as well. She's just the other side of Mr. Right but, obviously, is a woman. She's got a great body, a great personality, can hang with your friends and watch football for hours on end and she doesn't care if you call her or not. She can slam a beer and cook a turkey with no effort whatsoever. Miss Right is every man's dream. And that's all she is—a dream, a fantasy men have conjured up to escape reality.

There's nothing wrong with wanting someone perfect for you. It's when you want someone prefect that you tend to get in trouble. Women, like men, aren't prefect.

Sometimes they don't want to hang out with your friends and sometimes they might get upset because you forgot to call.

So, right now, ask yourself this: Am I waiting for Miss Right? Seriously, are you? And you do know that she doesn't exist, right? I hate to tell you, dude, but it's time to wake up and smell the espresso. If you are serious about meeting someone special, or dating some special girls, you have to get over your ideal Miss Right.

The problem might be that we've all been a little fooled by Hollywood. We forget that Hollywood manufactures dreams, not reality. Not only do they have romantic comedies for women displaying the perfect man, they give men the idea that there are perfect women in this world if only they could find them. And that's the rub right there—finding this perfect woman. It's like looking for a needle in a haystack when there was no needle in there to begin with.

Everyone buys into this ideal because it sounds so good. You get a cool chick, who is not only stacked, but allows you be you without any sort of responsibility. When this perfect woman never shows up, you end up feeling horrible about your life and wondering why no woman ever measures up to your ideal.

Movies aren't based in reality. But you think that if you wait long enough for this perfect woman, you will find her and live happily ever after. But you won't. She doesn't exist. But maybe the real reason you're waiting is because you see what's on the screen and feel like your life doesn't compare. It isn't as good as the characters in the movies and on TV. In fact, it's downright mundane. You might even think that your life is boring, so you need a girl like that to come in and liven things up a bit.

Many people have been so brainwashed by the media any "normal" person will have trouble cutting it with them.

Men want the perfect woman and women want the prefect man. So, each gender begins to turn their noses up at the opportunities in their lives and wait for something better. And they're going to be waiting a long, long time.

We've been told by the media to always stay young and never settle for less. Unfortunately, if no one ever settles, no one is ever going to get married, have kids and keep the universe going. If we never settle, we can never experience the true joy of being with someone who, simply, asks us how our day was.

So, it might be a good idea to come to terms with all this. There is no Miss Right, but there is a *Miss Right For You.* There is a woman who will love you for you. It's time to face facts and those facts are that women are human and they don't have superpowers and they can't live up to anyone's unrealistic expectations.

If you have these unrealistic expectations, it might be time to do a reality check. This could be a big reason you don't date as much as you'd like. This is about you making a conscious effort to get out there and get a good woman. It's about becoming the man women want and that means facing the reality of the situation: Women are just women, just as men are just men.

And isn't it time? Isn't it time to stop waiting and to start taking action? So, get over it and find yourself a real woman. It's definitely time to do that. Right?

Being worth it.

You might be beginning to think that a lot of the advice in this book centers on self-esteem. And you'd be right. Having good self-esteem—i.e. confidence—is what we're after. I believe that having these qualities helps a person get anything in life that they're after—from finding a great girl to getting the best pay.

One indicator that you are on the right track in life is knowing that you are worth it. This means that you know that the good things in life are within reach and, once you're able to obtain them, you can. The problem lies in the belief that you aren't worth it, that you don't deserve the best in life. If you think you're not worth it, if you think you don't deserve any of these great things life has to offer, you won't be. You have to feel like you are worth something in order for others to think you are, too. If you think you're not worth anything, you're fighting a losing battle.

If you have confidence, you don't think about things like whether or not you deserve something. You already know you do. And you know you do because you've put the time in for it. This doesn't mean that you think you're entitled to it just because you're so great; that's not what I'm talking about. But then again, maybe it is.

Have you ever noticed those people who seem like they're entitled? They always get the best out of life and that's because they don't expect any less. They do have a sense of entitlement but, then again, they always get what hey want. These people always seem to be happy, too, and hey're happy because they know that the things they want n life are obtainable and that they do deserve the best.

Do you think like this? If not, you might not be able to become the man women want. You might not be able to bring up that confidence you need in order to go through with dating the women you want to date. But all you have to do to turn this around is to recognize this hidden belief that you may have that you're not worthy and that you don't deserve the best. If you can recognize it, then you can do something about it. Then you get it out of your system, step over it and start living the life you want.

So, what you have to do is get it in your mind that you are worth it. You are worth a pretty girl taking the time to get to know you. You are worth having a better job, car, house or whatever. If you can start to believe this and get over your low self-esteem, you can begin to obtain all that might have seen elusive.

I think most problems in life start with your attitude. If you carry around the attitude that you're not worth anything and that you're a low human being, so you shall be. You have to overcome this in order to be more open to the opportunities that will come your way. And, if you can do this, you can get over the desperation. You can overcome the feeling of lack and of doing without. You can let things go.

Once you can do this, women will want to get to know you better. It's inevitable. Being the man women want means being worth it. If they see you as having worth, they're going to want to latch onto you. However, if you don't see yourself as having worth, they never will, either.

Get it into your mind that you are one cool dude. You're hot, man! You're a rock star! You are worth some chick taking the time to talk to you and go out with you. You are worth having them flirt with you and getting to

know you better. Don't be afraid to ask for what you wan
and if it's a hot chick, then so be it. You want a hot chick
And you deserve one, too.

Being worth it also means being choosy. You don't have
to stick with a girl that might make you feel bad abou
yourself. You have a right to be picky. But this doesn't mean
to be *too* picky. This doesn't mean to tear a woman down
once you get her and bail at the first sign of imperfection
Just understanding that you are a hot commodity and
tapping into what you have to offer—being a good guy who
cares or whatever—is all you need to be worth it. And al
this entails is that you start believing you are worth the
effort.

And you are, you know?

Desperate is as desperate does.

I know we've covered being desperate several times in this book already, but I want to touch on a few more things before we move on. So, let's get it out of the way: Don't be desperate.

This might not even apply to you. I hope it doesn't. But if it does, you might want to consider the reality of what it's like to be desperate. I have seen a lot of men who will put up with a lot of headaches from women just because they're afraid of being alone or whatever. It's pretty obvious why these guys do this—they're insecure and don't think they deserve any better. And this makes them desperate and allows women to walk all over them and treat them in a not so nice way.

There is no need for you to ever be desperate. It will cause nothing but problems.

If you want to be the man women want, you have to get over being desperate. Ironically enough, once you stop being desperate, women will usually start giving you the respect you deserve. I know where the desperation comes from and it comes from a sense of feeling inadequate combined with the panic of being alone. It's a pretty simple combination that amounts to a lot of misery. Of course you don't want to end up alone but that doesn't mean to get desperate and allow women to walk all over you. It means that you're aware that you need to do something about your situation and that you'd like to eventually get married and, perhaps, have a family. Hey, that's great! These are the things most normal people want. And if you put in the effort to obtain these goals, you will probably end up getting what you want. But if you're desperate about it, you're probably going to end up with someone who walks all over you.

Understand that the woman you choose will be a big influence on how the rest of your life turns out. If this woman doesn't respect you to begin with, she's probably going to nag you all the time about everything in the world once you're together. Do you want that? I didn't think so.

Of course, this doesn't mean to pass on every woman you meet because you might fear she will walk all over you. No. It just means letting her know to begin with what you will and won't put up with. This also means that if you do start dating a great girl, don't push yourself on her. Be cool about it, hold back and allow the relationship to evolve at its own pace. If you bug someone too much in the beginning, they will eventually find a way out of the relationship. If you call more than a few times a week during the early stages of the relationship, you will come off as being desperate. Then she will start treating you bad in hopes you will break it off with her so she won't have to go to the trouble herself. Harsh truth, but that's just the reality of the situation.

So, just think about how desperation might be playing a role in your dating style. If it is, it's time to nip it in the bud and start believing that you don't have to be desperate in order to date a hot babe.

Tips on successful dating.

It's pretty simple to become the man women want. It's also not that hard to have success in dating. But, in order to do this, you have to define what you want, what you are willing to put up with and the lengths you're willing to go. Or, on the other hand, what you're *not* willing to put up with and the lengths you *won't* go.

Can't think of anything off the top of your head? Never fear. I have a list.

To become the man women want, it's a good idea to…

- Have boundaries. What will you put up with and what won't you put up with? What if she's perpetually late? What if she hates your friends? What if she makes fun of your dog?
- Communicate your boundaries. Once you establish your boundaries, don't be afraid to let her know about them. This lets her know you won't be anybody's doormat. Now, if you want to be someone's booty call, that's entirely up to you.
- Establish what you want out of a woman, out of a relationship and out of life. Write it out. If it's a home and family, good for you. If it's to play the field, then okay. However, defining this is a must in order to achieve it.
- You have to have confidence. When a guy is confident in himself, he's the man! A guy with

confidence never reeks of desperation and doesn't fear leaving the party alone. He just goes with the flow. A confident man doesn't need a woman in his life, but never rules out the possibility of dating one.

- Watch your drinking. Drinking too much can make fools out of even the best men. So, be careful not to use alcohol not as a social stimulant.

- Keep in mind that every woman you meet might not be looking to settle down. So, if marriage and commitment scare you, you're in good company because it scares a lot of women, too. However, if this is what you're looking for, don't get too upset when you find someone who doesn't want the same thing. Just keep trying until you do.

- Relationships are work. Any one you might get involved with will be work. You have to be willing to work at relationships.

- Never, ever be afraid to get out of a bad relationship. Even if she's the prettiest thing you've ever laid eyes on. If you end up marrying this chick, she will probably make you miserable. If you can't live without her, just be prepared.

These are just some suggestions. You might already have a list yourself and it might be somewhat different than this one. That's okay. You can add or take away the things that apply to you and your personal dating style. The point is to open your mind so you can expand your horizons. This is a simple guideline, but understand these are the things that can help make you successful at dating. And that's what we're after, buddy.

The pretty ones are always the craziest.

For some reason, crazy always comes hand in hand with pretty. Have you ever noticed this? The most attractive women always seem to have a screw loose somewhere. But that's what makes them so interesting. Right?

But you men just love them, don't you? Crazy girls are just the bomb! They can stir it up and keep it fun. The crazy girl is the female equivalent to the bad boy. Women love bad boys and you men love your crazy girls.

I tend to agree. Crazy girls *are* interesting. Sure, she's fun. She's exciting! But what if she gets a crazy idea about burning down someone's house or knocking over a liquor store? She could, you know. They don't call her crazy for no reason.

If you are the sort of guy who is very attracted to the crazy girl, it might be time to ask yourself why. I can understand that you might want to "save" her, but my question here would be: Why not save yourself? If you get too overly involved with a crazy girl, she is going to suck a lot of life and time away from you. And she can't help it. That's just the way she is. As fun and as exciting as she can be—in the beginning—it will start to wear thin after a while. Because crazy is as crazy does. And crazy does a lot of crazy stuff.

Finding yourself in a relationship with a crazy girl will do one of two things: Give you the excitement you need or the heart attack you don't.

The only problem with dating a crazy girl is that you will waste a lot of time in a relationship like this and it will emotionally—sometimes financially—bankrupt you. And it will keep you off the market for better women. Better women won't go near you if they think you're involved with a crazy girl. They will stay away because once a crazy girl becomes a crazy ex-girlfriend, she will drive both of you out of your minds. Therefore, she will haunt any new relationship you might have.

Of course, I am not saying all good looking women are crazy. No, no. I am saying that you guys sometimes just see the pretty and not the crazy. Of course, you know she's a little off when you start seeing her, but damn it! She's so pretty! You can't take your eyes off her. Understandable. But what happens when the fun and excitement wears off? You're stuck with her. And all the crazy things she does.

So, is she worth it?

Usually, not. But give the girl some credit. She's just doing what come naturally. However, if you can avoid her my advice would be to do that very thing. And if you've already got her in your life, just be careful. If you're lucky she'll get bored with you and go on to torture someone else.

Women are not bitches.

One thing that will stand in your way of becoming the man women want is a bad attitude. And if you go into any situation involving women where you have the attitude that all women are bitches, you're going to fail.

Sure, sure, I know some women are bitches. It comes with the territory. I also know that some women *can* be bitches. No surprise there. But, mostly, women want what men want and that's love. They want to be loved for who they are—bad moods and all. This doesn't mean they hate men and it doesn't mean they would rather stay single for the rest of eternity than to succumb to a man, it just means that, sometimes, they get tired and frustrated. Some of them just get tired of playing men's games and some of them get tired of being the casualty some guy's commitment phobia. This, among other things, can make them a bit hard-nosed and difficult to deal with.

As we all know, dating can be hard. It can be hard to get out there and try, try again. But if we never attempt to do it, then we have nothing to look forward to in life but the new fall television schedule. A bit sad, isn't it?

The point is if you want to be the man that women want, you have to like women. Sure, you don't have to put up with bitches that make you feel terrible about yourself or whatever. But being with a woman will entail some overlooking of her mood swings from time to time.

Of course, there are those women out there who think the worse you treat a guy, the better he will be to you. I think they call this "be mean to keep him keen" or something to that effect. And, yes, this might work with some men—perhaps those with a masochistic side? However, most men don't want a woman who puts them or their friends down and never has a good thing to say about anyone. They don't want someone who constantly picks at them or makes their lives miserable. They don't like to be made to feel inferior and they certainly don't like to be yelled at.

All of this is completely and totally understandable.

But on the other side of this, do you really want a mousy woman who will sit in the corner and never say a word in her defense? Do you really want someone you can push around and do your bidding? Of course you don't. You want to be on equal playing ground with whatever woman you choose to date or even marry. In other words, you want to respect her.

Sure, you don't want a woman who won't stand up for herself, but, on the other hand, you don't want one who screams about your socks or the toilet seat. Am I right? It seems that being in a situation like this is like being between a rock and a hard place.

The only way around this is compromise. Things can be balanced out. One way to do this is to view the bitch angle from a different viewpoint. You might need to know that women who are bitches and who put others down do so because they feel inferior, not superior as you might think. They think that by belittling others, they can put themselves on a higher level. They don't realize how much they alienate others and that's because deep-down, they're hurting. And yes, they are. Someone or something has happened to these women to hurt them deeply. You might not ever realize this because they're probably hiding their feelings, maybe even from themselves.

But this woman isn't like every single woman out there. Just because a woman stands up for herself and doesn't take crap from others doesn't make her a bitch. These women can assert themselves without sounding harsh. However, if you, as the guy who might be on the receiving end of this, misunderstand it, you might be apt to put this one in the dreaded category of the bitch. And what a loss you'd have on your hands then.

This is why it's so important not to paint every woman you see with the same brush. *Not all women are bitches.* Sure, some women are mean, vile shrews. This doesn't make them evil; it just makes them look bad. However, some women are just plain bitches who assert themselves when necessary. Learning to distinguish between these two will be a major factor in your dating success.

So, it might be worth mentioning to overlook when you can and to stand up for yourself when necessary. All women aren't bitches but if you think they are, you are just cheating yourself out of a lot of good loving. Besides that, if a woman just happens to be mean to you, it might just be PMS. And God knows there's nothing right a man can do when a woman is in the throes of PMS. Best to get out of her way and let her cool off until she comes back to her senses.

The girl with the commitment issues.

Let's say you've met the perfect girl. She's everything you want. You are *in luv*, as they say. Good for you! However, things start to turn a little, shall we say…uneasy between the two of you. What happens once you've got that great girl and you're in love but she suddenly starts acting a little…? I don't know… Aloof. What happens when you can feel her pulling back some, not wanting to go out as much?

Well, it's entirely up to you what to do, but first off, you need to decide if this is a relationship you want to keep. If not, let her go. Big deal. If it is, however, a relationship you want to keep there is something you can do to get her interested in you once again. And all it entails is that you suddenly become unavailable.

What you may have on your hands is a girl with commitment issues. Maybe she's missing the single lifestyle and her friends. So what? You've heard that saying, "If you love someone, set them free…" Blah, blah, blah. And that's what you do. You set her free. But while she's out there being all free, you're out there, too. You become suddenly unavailable. And how do you do that? It's easy. Just start pulling away. Pull back some. Just a little to let her know that you're not there all the time anymore. Not so much to make her think you're getting disinterested, but enough to et her miss you. This lets her know she's not the only game n town. This lets her know you have a life, too.

This may be hard for you because you probably really ike this chick. However, if you don't do something, you night end up losing her forever. If you're afraid she might hink you don't like her, then you're at risk for becoming ner doormat. And that is a position you never want to find yourself in with a woman. Never be her doormat! No matter now good looking she is or how good in bed she is. This will only lead to you losing self respect and a man without self respect is like a dog without a cold nose. Well, that might not be the best analogy, but you get my point.

Keep in mind that if she starts pulling away and you start chasing her, she might just break up with you. This means she wasn't falling in love anyway. But never chase ner. If she wants to run away, give her your frequent flyer miles. So what? She's not the only woman in the world, man! Get over her and move on.

Know that if you spend all your free time with any woman, you are pretty much asking for trouble. You will kill even the best relationship. People need their space. People need time apart. If you're all over her all the time, she will start to think you're crowding her and it won't be long before the ball and chain starts to weigh heavy on her.

But if you pull back a little, she might start to think she's not been acting right. She might start missing you and all the fun you once had. She might see you for the good guy you are. If you "forget" to return her call a few times, she might think you're seeing someone else. This will make her very jealous and if it does, she should be back in your arms in no time.

So, all you have to do is don't return a call every once in while, tell her occasionally that you can't go out because you have "other plans" and "forget" to meet her a time or two. And when she asks what happened? Just say, "Oh, no did I do that? I must have got the dates mixed up o something. Sorry."

It all becomes about not being someone's bitch. It al becomes about being "unavailable" to someone else every waking minute of the day. Once you do this, once you le her know you can get on without her just fine, more thar likely, she will straighten up. Once she sees that she's abou to lose something great, she might just come back home. mean, if she's already pulling back from you, what could i hurt for you to do the same? You're just beating her to the punch.

Now, keep in mind that this might backfire and she might just go ahead and pull the plug on the relationship (*Remember that this is a risk that involves rea consequences.*) If so, then she was going to do it anyway, no matter what you do. And if that happens, she was neve going to make you happy in the first place. No big deal. Jus set her free.

You sexy thang!

Everything in life is about attitude and I think that's what we've been discussing pretty much throughout this book. If you want to be the man women want, it all starts with you believing you can become that man. It's all about your attitude and how you use it to your advantage. However, if you waver on this even just a little, you won't be the man women want. You'll be the man women avoid.

You don't want that now, do you?

Obviously, women don't approach men as much as men approach women. We all know it's your "job" to do the approaching or send the signal. But what if you could have it both ways? What if you could approach a woman and even have them approach you? What if you could have your cake and eat it too?

I think you can.

The key factor to becoming the man women want, as I've been saying all along, is confidence, confidence, confidence! Women absolutely love a man who displays confidence. This lets them know that if he's confident in himself enough to approach them, he's got enough confidence not to let them get away. This means, he's got enough confidence to buy them a drink. This means he's got enough confidence to ask for their number and use it to call them later in the week.

When you exhibit confidence, this lets women know that you haven't let life bog you down. You're just out having fun and that's all. This also lets them know you don't have any issues that might cramp their style if and when they decide to get together with you. Women, like most everyone else, don't like to be around a guy with too many issues. If you've got too many issues, it might be best to take care of them before you figuratively take it out on the dance floor. But if you come to meet them with a clean slate, all the better. More fun for all!

We've already discussed how you can be more confident in earlier chapters. But I will reiterate that you have to get it into your mind that you are worth it. You are worth some chick taking a chance on. You are worth a girl taking the time to chat it up with you. You're just worth it.

Keep in mind that women like to keep men guessing. That's why they play all those head games with you. It's fun for them to see you squirm. Women think if they lay everything out on the table all at once, men will run for the door. Women are afraid of looking too needy and they certainly don't want to look desperate. This may be why some are a little off-putting at first. They want you to want them but they don't want you to know they're thinking that. It's called having "mystery." But men may take is as being "elusive."

Is it any wonder, then, that the dating game is so skewed? No, but you shouldn't let this stop you.

So, this brings us to our point. When you're out and about, it's good to carry a "just don't care" attitude. This will make you sexy to women. So, what you have to do is that whenever you see a chick you think is hot, throw her smile but then go right back to doing whatever you were doing— shooting pool, talking with a friend, whatever. It's best not to be too eager, especially at first. This will spark her interest and you might be surprised when she finds an excuse to come up to you and start a conversation. You might fall out of your seat when it's her that sends you a drink.

It could happen, you know?

This is why I said earlier that you can have your cake and eat it, too, especially, if you are willing to hold back a little and not act too eager. You can approach women and you can have them approach you. It works both ways. So, whenever it does happen, just be yourself. Be your sexy, confident self. When she comes over, say "hello" and smile like you're glad she's taking the time. When you go over to her, smile and say "hello" and know that she's going to be glad you took the time. And that's the key—take your time! Ease yourself into it. Don't think that just because you're in front of her you have to make a fool out of yourself. If you can't think of anything to say, just say, with a disarming smile, "This is kinda awkward, isn't it?" And then watch her relax and maybe even smile. Because it can be awkward. Meeting anyone for the first time *is* awkward. But do your best to keep it light and fun. If she knows how fun you can be, she will want to hang out with you more.

So, if you can act like you just don't care, you will pretty much become unstoppable. And you know why? Because you don't care! Your life isn't dependent on one date from one girl. And that means, you will begin to open yourself up to more possibilities than you ever imagined.

Funny how that works.

What happens now?

Let's say you've met a great girl at a dinner, bar, club or whatever. You're into her and, as far as you can tell, she's into you. However, after a while, the conversation begins to wane just a little. What to do? It's simple. Just excuse yourself. If she asks where you're going, just say you need to make a call or something.

Taking a break will allow you to think of things to talk about and to relax a bit and get a little perspective on how you want to proceed. Now, this may seem like a bummer, but if you go back in and she's with someone else, don't freak out. Let her go and this will allow another to take her place. Never get hung up on one girl. *Never!* If the first sees that you've moved on, she's going to want back in the picture. And it will be up to you to make that decision.

Don't forget that you can get what you want. You just can't make someone like you. No matter how hard you try, you can never, ever *make* someone want you. But you can let them know that they've missed out on something. And when they feel like that, they will usually want to come back over to you to see what's up. This is why it's important not to get hung up on just one girl. When one sees that you can live without her, then she will see the value in you.

Like I have said, by being willing to let one go, you are allowing another to take her place. It's that simple. And once you do that, she might just want to be your number one. She might just see she was about to lose something great. And women hate to lose a man to another woman, just let me tell you. Even if she's not that interested in you to begin with, she will hate it when another woman makes time for you. That's a big secret not many guys know. I tell you this to enlighten you and, also, so you can use it to your advantage, but not to her detriment. So, use with caution.

Also, by being willing to walk away from her, you are presenting her with a challenge. She might think she's the one who can't think of anything to say. Remember that women can be shy and tongue-tied too. Men don't have the market covered on this, that's for sure. Keep in mind that no one likes rejection of any sort, so if she sees she's about to "lose" you, she might perk up or she might just be honest and say, "I'm sorry, I'm not good at meeting new people." And this can happen to the best of us. We get all hyped up to meet new people but when presented with one, we suddenly turn shy. Keep that in mind when you're meeting women and it might help you to relax a little bit more.

Remember, you don't have to settle on the first girl you meet and talk to. There may be things about this girl you're not comfortable with and, if so, be willing to let go and move on. This is where not being desperate will come in handy. If you know you can get another girl—and you can— then there's no reason to proceed with one who drives you crazy, and not with lust either.

If you think you're coming on too strong...

I know it can be hard once you meet someone you'd like to get to know better not to come on too strong. You might have a fear that if she doesn't know you're alive, she could get away for good and you'll never see her again. This is why it's so important to be self-aware enough to know when you're about to do something foolish.

When you go out, just remember to keep it light. If you feel yourself starting to become too aggressive or get too hung-up on one particular girl, cool off for a bit. This is just insecurity guiding you to make foolish decisions. So, take a breather, get a drink, go outside, do whatever you have to do in order not to come on too strong. Just relax. You don't have to be in charge right now. You can let go of control. It's okay. It won't be the end of the world if this one gets away.

Remember the less you seem to care, the more women will want you. And the more you seem to care? The more they will want to get away from you. It's kind of like reverse psychology. This isn't to say, of course, that once you start dating that you can't show you care. No, no, no. It just means you don't have to show you care until you've actually got some sign she's interested in you. And you will know the signs she's interested. And what are they?

The signs she's diggin' ya:

- She smiles at you.
- She asks you for the time.
- She asks what you're drinking and points at it.
- She compliments your clothing, watch, shoes, etc.
- She says hello out of the blue.
- She touches your arm.
- She throws her head back and laughs at a joke.
- She pats your leg.

These are just a few signs, but I think you get the gist. The point is, you will probably know when she's interested. It won't be too hard to see, unless you're just completely oblivious to any human interaction. And I'm guessing you're not.

Girls' night out.

There's a lot of confusion about why women are out in clubs and at parties or whatever. Some guys think they just show up to find a bad boy or whatever. Some think they're just there to hang out with friends. But why do women really go out? It's got a whole lot less to do with women than you'd think.

Mostly a girls' night out is about meeting and talking to and sometimes going home with men. Like I said, it's not that much to do with other women. You have to keep in mind that when women are out and about at clubs, parties or whatever, they, too, are looking for potential mates. They're not just there to hang with their girlfriends. They can see those chicks anytime. But when they've taken the time to dress up and go out, it's usually because they've got men on their mind.

The point of this is this: Don't get intimidated when you see a group of women together. They're probably bored with each other and wish some man—any man!—would talk to them. Why not be that man? Why not approach the group with a disarming smile and ask, "What's up, ladies?" Then see what kind of reaction you get. If it's relieved smiles, you've just hit the jackpot. If it's rolled eyes and sighs, it might be a good idea to retreat. But remember nothing ventured, nothing gained.

However, keep in mind that just because women do, indeed, go out with friends in order to meet men, they're not just there to get laid. They are more than likely looking for someone to date.

Sure, there are some women who are on the prowl, so to speak. These women might just be divorced or looking to cheat on their men, or whatever. I say, always use caution. If you hook up with someone who has a jealous ex, you might be in for a world of pain. I'd suggest always asking questions before going the extra mile with one of these chicks. Sure, you might get laid, but if it costs you an arm, literally, then it's not going to be worth it.

The point of all this is to let you know what while women in groups may put off the vibe they're just out "having a good time," more than likely, they won't mind changing their plans if the "right" man comes along. So, why not be that right man? The key is to always be open to whatever new possibility presents itself. That's the important thing.

Hey, good looking!

We all know that becoming the man women want entails being confident. That's a given. Finding that confidence will enable you to have the ability to get out there and find the woman of your dreams. And one way to build confidence is to look your best.

It's a given that women like men who look good. Women like men who look their best. And looking your best is nothing more than tweaking what you already have. It does not mean buying out the stores or running up a credit card bill, so don't worry. This isn't about how much you spend as much as spending wisely. And if you don't want to spend anything, then that's entirely up to you. However, if you can get over your hesitancy about getting dressed up, you will pave the way to attract more women.

And what does it matter? I know many of you think that a woman should love you for you. And she should. And she will—once she gets to know you. But you have to have something for her to latch onto and if you look your best, she will see that you care enough to put the effort in. And that means she will be attracted to you all the more.

If you are feeling any sort of resistance to this chapter, then feel free to skip it. If it's not that important to you to go the extra mile, then so be it. But I'd be willing to bet that while you don't think you should have to look nice, you sure want the women you meet to do so. Am I right? And if this is true, isn't that being just a little hypocritical? Just think of t this way: Are you going to be attracted to some chick in a gunny sack dress or to the hot babe in a form-fitting outfit? I think the answer is pretty obvious.

You have to understand that people are attracted to attractive people. That's just the way it works. This doesn't mean that you have to go out and have plastic surgery or anything. That is not that I am saying to do at all. It simply means that you take what you have now and you make it better. It is about looking your best. And, again, if you are feeling resistance on this, why not stop right now and ask yourself why you are so resistant? Is it because you fear change? Do you think that someone is trying to change you? We are all resistant to change in some form or another but if you are so resistant that you get stuck and can't move forward, it might be time to do a little soul searching.

If you want to be the man women want, you have to get yourself unstuck in your old ways and get out there and get to it. No one is going to do this for you. No one can wave a magic wand over you and give you what you want. Being the man women want does entail being attractive to the opposite sex.

I know some of you are probably thinking, "But it shouldn't matter!" No, it shouldn't, should it? It shouldn't matter how you dress or what you look like. All women should love you for you. And here's the kicker—they will! But you have to first be attractive to them in order for them to do so. If you can't take that little bit of truth here, then how are you going to take it from someone in real life? If it makes you that uncomfortable, then don't do it. But this book is for men who want to have better dating lives. It's for men who aren't so resistant to change that they would get upset if someone dared mentioned that they aren't absolutely perfect. If you are such a man, then read on. And if not, ask yourself why.

Ask yourself this: What is holding me back? What is th
fear here? And what you might find is that you have som
deep-seated insecurity. And that's okay! Many people do
Insecurity can make the best of us lose it from time to time
Insecurity is also a sneaky little bitch. She rears her head a
any opportunity to make us feel unworthy and foolish. Isn'
it time, though, to tell her to take a hike? If you can find th
source of your insecurity, then you can overcome mos
anything. Find it, deal with it and move on.

And in the meanwhile, why not look your best? B
putting in the effort, you are telling yourself that you ar
worth it, you deserve the best and you are open to change
And if you're not open, then nothing can help you. It is onl
by letting go of control that you can move forward.

Keep in mind that no one is trying to control you
And—newsflash—no one wants to, either! We all have ou
own problems to deal with and trying to control someone i
a waste of time. Why would anyone extend the effort t
control another? It's beyond my realm of comprehension
But what I do know is that if you're a guy who wants a gir
then you gotta do something about it. If you want to dat
and be wanted, you have to look your best. I understan
this. And maybe you should, too.

So, if you're a guy who wants to be the man wome
want and you want to look your best, I'm going to tell yo
how. I am going to tell you how to look more attractive t
women. And, as you read this, just take what you can us
and leave the rest. Tweak it for your individual preference
Make your own rules about how you dress, but use thes
guidelines. I know all this won't apply to every single one c
you, so just take what you can use and forget the rest.

While you might want to conform to the standar
average Joe look, never be afraid to stand out a little. Thi
doesn't mean to overdo it with gold chains and Italia

leather loafers. This means, dress age-appropriately and keep your style simple and up to date.

Here's a list of things to think about:
- How stylish are your clothes?
- Is your weight about where it should be for your body type and height?
- Do you have a scraggly beard or goatee?
- Do you dress too young—or even too old—for your age?
- Is your hair going crazy and in all directions?
- Are your nails trim and clean?

Really think about all this. Consider it. You want to be the best you can be so the women out there will look at you first and not some other jerk. More importantly, you don't want them to not overlook you. If you don't stand out a little by being one of the best dressed guys in the bar, then they'll keep looking until they find him. And that's one reason those guys always go home with the hottie—they look good! That's why women want them. It doesn't take Einstein to figure this one out. It does matter what you look like. It's a hard truth, but if you can accept it, then you can free up that space in your mind to do something about it so that you are not out of the game before you even get a foot in.

In essence: The better you look, the more likely you attract better women. And, no, we are not talking handsome actor looks, either. We are just talking about looking the best *you* can. Everyone has lots of good qualities. You simply build on those you have. You might be naturally charming or a good flirt. Maybe you can fix lots of stuff or know how to hook up stereos. Whatever you have, you build on it. And by taking the guessing game out of how you're dressed—by dressing well and appropriately—you give women the opportunity to get to know the real you.

Now looking good does not involve obsessing. This should be a simple, easy process. Don't make it hard, either. It doesn't take a rocket scientist to figure these things out. All you need is to clean up a little. Trim your beard and maybe get a haircut. Buy a nice, simple outfit and good shoes.

It is not hard to take what you've got and make it work for you. It all begins by looking in the mirror and seeing what you can improve on. If you become the best you can be, it will give you more confidence to get out there and meet women.

Here are the things you might want to consider improving on:

- Weight. Many people could stand to lose a few pounds. No big deal. If this is you, then just lose a few pounds. It doesn't take much and what works in reality isn't some crazy diet plan that entails you weighing your food or eating a pound of bacon. What works is cutting back on your calories and exercising. It's really simple and easy. Never starve yourself, just watch how much you eat and don't ever overeat. If you do that, you will lose weight. There's no way you can't. (Be sure to check with your doctor before beginning any weight loss program.)

- Hair. One of the first things a woman looks at is your hair. Is it messy in a cool guy way or just plain messy? If it's the latter, it's time to clean it up. Get a haircut. It's that simple. Men are lucky because they don't have to put too much time or effort into their hair. Just make sure it's neat and trim and looks good for the shape of your face. If you are unsure, go to a stylist and ask them to make suggestions on what you can do.

- Nails. Many men overlook the importance of nice, clean nails. Don't overlook this! Keep your nails clean, trim and buffed. You don't have to do anything else.
- Cologne. Never overdose on cologne. Just a touch is all you need.
- Clothes. Just buy things that are in style and of good quality. With men, and again, you're lucky this way, it's the quality of clothes that matter, not the quantity. So you can get away with just buying a few key pieces to amp up your current wardrobe. The main idea here is for your clothing to be age appropriate and current.

One more thing. Never go out of the house looking sloppy. You do realize that women are everywhere, even at the grocery store, right? So, it's important to look your best at all times. Looking your best will make others take notice of you. It's that simple.

That's about it. It wasn't too painful, was it? Keep in mind, that once you feel like you're worth it and get over your insecurity issues, you can be more confident in your approach to women and dating. And confidence is what we're after, people.

Listen to yourself!

Earlier, we covered insecurity issues, but I think it warrants going over again. If you have insecurity issues, they will, inevitably, taint everything you do.

So, how do you know if you have insecurity issues? Just listen to yourself. What is your inner dialogue? What do you say to yourself? When you look in the mirror, do you cringe and pick apart your faults—perceived or otherwise? Do you constantly put yourself down? Do you tell yourself you're not good looking enough or successful enough or can never lose weight? Do you get angry with others when they offer helpful criticism? Do you ever explode with rage over a perceived slight? If you answered yes to any of these questions, you may just have insecurity issues.

You need to understand that no one but you can "fix" this. One of the simplest and easiest fixes is to evaluate yourself and your life. Sure, you might not be at the top right now, but does that mean you're at the bottom? Probably not. So, evaluate yourself and then think of ways to improve on what you've got.

Another good way to overcome insecurity issues is to stop looking for others to complete you. This means, stop looking for a woman to swoop into your life and make everything okay. You have to know—and believe—that you are okay *as-is*. You don't need someone to complete you. Sure, it would be nice to have someone *complement* you, but that's entirely different than thinking there is a part of you that is missing and until you find this one woman you won't be whole. You are whole right now. There's nothing wrong with you.

And that's the thing to keep in mind. That's the biggie—really and truly knowing and understanding that there is nothing wrong with you. You weren't born with a chip missing or whatever. *You are okay.* Sure, we've been discussing ways to improve upon yourself, but that's entirely different school of thought than thinking there's something wrong with you. This should not be misconstrued, either. Knowing you are okay, with or without a hottie, is what you're after. But also knowing that if you improve on what you've already got, your chances have more than doubled of getting what you want.

Keep in mind that everyone can improve upon themselves, even those people we view as already being perfect. We are humans and humans are always evolving. It's when we get stuck into destructive thinking that we get tripped up. But if you have basic insecurity issues, you may just be afraid to change. Insecurity can be a tough emotion to deal with. It can trip you up and hold you back and even make you perceive things the wrong way. For instance, someone might compliment you on your jacket or whatever, but if you have insecurity issues, you might take it the wrong way and think they're making fun of you.

Do you get what I'm saying? There's nothing wrong with you, it's just your insecurity making you feel that way. And if you constantly feel insecure and not "as good" as anyone else, then there's no way you can become the man women want. You've got too many issues already! And because of this, even if a great girl offered you a chance to get to know her, you might find something wrong with it.

So, the only way out of this is to first recognize that you have insecurity issues. Secondly, you need to make a valiant effort to stop letting your insecurity guide your life. And, lastly, you should try to find ways to improve upon yourself so that the insecurity just eventually fades.

It's not that hard to do, either. It's mostly listening to what you say to yourself and then correcting yourself. If you say, "I am a big, fat slob of a human being," then you would simply turn it around and say instead, "I am big. But then again, I am trying to improve that. It takes time and I am taking the time to do it."

This is quite easy to do. But most importantly, start listening to yourself. Listen to what you say to yourself and once you can do that, just start overriding the negative with a positive. Soon enough, it will become second nature and your confidence will soar. And that's what we're after.

Watch your mouth.

There are a few things you should never say to a woman upon meeting, on the first date or, well, ever. If you've ever witnessed another guy saying these things, I'm sure you've cringed. And if it's you who been doing this, it's time to stop. Now, these are just a few examples and the idea is to not say anything vulgar or too personal. Ready?

Here goes:
- How far do you go on a first date?
- Are those real?
- Do the curtains match the rug?

No, no and no. Don't even go there. Ever. Even if you're thinking it, it doesn't mean you have to say it. Learn how to edit yourself. Think about what you say before it comes out of your mouth, especially when you first meet someone.

If you say things like this to women, all it makes them want to do is punch you. I won't sugarcoat this. You have to realize that they are not going to get the joke. If you have to say things like this, just say them to your friends and have a good chuckle. But if you feel the need to do this, maybe there's another issue going on and that issue is probably a lack of respect for women.

Think about this: How can you charm her if she hates you? You can't. So, make it a policy to keep these sorts of thoughts *inside* your head and never allow them *out* of your mouth. Give women the respect they deserve. They are human beings, just like you. Their feelings do get hurt and when some guy smarmily asks if their breasts are real, they know they're being degraded.

On the other hand, I think many men who do this sort of thing have an even deeper issue at hand, other than having a lack of respect for women. I think they don't respect themselves. I think they go into a situation with most women thinking they're already dead in the water before they even open their mouths. It's almost like a defense mechanism. They think, "She's going to shoot me down anyway, so let me go ahead and throw out the first insult before she gets a chance."

And the sad thing about this is, she might not even be thinking along these lines! She *might* be interested in you before you say something awful like that to her. But once those words are out of your mouth, all bets are off. She's going to think of you as the guy who put her down.

The point is mutual respect. If you want respect, you have to give it. Always go into a new situation with an open mind. Always give a woman the respect she deserves. If you say things like this, you're letting fear of rejection control you. And we've already talked about that. Let the fear go and let it dissolve.

But mostly, respect yourself enough not to make a fool out of yourself. Respect yourself enough to know that it's never appropriate to throw mud in someone's face figuratively speaking. If you keep doing things like this, you might just come across a woman who can and will tear you down. And you don't want that. What you want is to feel confident. So, never put yourself in a position where someone can get a cheap shot at you just because you left yourself open to it.

I mean, what's the fun in that? Why not stay home and play video games? You're out and about because you want to meet someone. Right? If you just came out to put someone down, then why not just stay home?

Let me ask you this: What sort of high do you get out of putting someone down? Do you really feel that badly about yourself that you have to put someone down in order to feel better about yourself? If so, then this is an issue you definitely need to reconcile. So, keep it in check when you want to throw out a remark like the ones listed. See how your body feels. Do you feel anxious? Do you feel like you're being put down in some way? Just listen to your thoughts and how your body feels. And then sort through those feelings. I'd be willing to bet it's nothing more than insecurity rearing its ugly little head. So, get your insecurity in check and get on with your night. And never, ever, let it keep you from trying to make a connection.

Rejection is a bitch. Get over it.

If you can get over your fear of rejection, there will be no stopping you from becoming the man women want. Granted, rejection is hard. No one likes being rejected. But to get hung up on it only means that you are not seeing the forest for the trees. Rejection is part of dating. In fact, it's a sad truth of life. However, if you can get over it, you can start living the life you want.

Remember we talked about the feelings of not being *good enough*? When you think of yourself as lesser than others, then you put out this vibe that you are. People can and will pick up on this. And once this happens, you kind of get in this cycle of *being* rejected. Soon enough, it's everywhere you turn and it seems as though you can't escape it.

It's like this: Once you start *expecting* rejection, you fall into the trap of always *being* rejected. This is why confidence is so important. Getting over your fear of rejection will lead to a more confident you. And even if you do end up getting rejected, you won't let it trip you up.

If it were only that easy, right? The fear of being rejected stops many people dead in their tracks. They get so afraid of being rejected, they stop attempting to do anything. They think, "Well, why should I? They're just going to reject me anyway." They refuse to put themselves out there for fear of embarrassment. And that's the thing that makes rejection sting the most, isn't it? That embarrassment. That humiliation. These aren't easy emotions to contend with and this is why many people stop putting themselves out there. The fear of being humiliated is overpowering. Why bother with it at all?

So, we can ascertain that rejection is pretty much fear of embarrassment, right? Sure. It doesn't take a genius to figure that one out. And nobody likes that red-hot stinging feeling of being mortified. I don't like it. You don't like it. Nobody likes it.

Unfortunately, it's part of dating. Sorry to tell you this. Rejection is part of dating. But if you can get over your fear of it, you can start to date more often and date better than ever before. Think of all those guys who've already given up because some chick dismissed them ten or twenty or however many years ago. He's taken himself off the market. He's let this one incident take him completely off the market. And for what? Why? Because he can't stand the feelings that being rejected gave him.

Rejection is just par for the course in dating. It's just part of the process. If you can't handle rejection, firstly, ask yourself why and then, secondly, ask yourself if you should even be *trying* to date since you can't handle the feeling of being rejected.

And that's all it is, fellas, it's a feeling. It's not a particularly pleasant feeling, but it's just a feeling. It's when you get tripped up on this feeling that you start to lose confidence. The idea is to not let it trip you up.

On the other end of the spectrum is acceptance. Every human being craves and needs acceptance. It's a basic human need. We need to feel accepted. We want to be wanted. And once we feel some acceptance, our confidence begins to grow. And as this happens, we experience more freedom from these unpleasant feelings and can begin to expect better things out of life.

But, unfortunately, getting that acceptance we need ca be hard. But you have to keep trying. There's no other wa around it. You have to keep putting yourself out there, ever if all you think you'll ever get is rejected. And if you kee doing this, more than likely, you will finally find someon who will accept you. And once that happens, guess what Even more people will begin to accept you. And then, a long last, you will have that acceptance you've wanted.

Before all this can happen, why don't you just d yourself a big favor and accept yourself? Why not jus embrace everything about yourself? Embrace all your flaw and all your quirks along with your positive attributes. I you can begin to be more accepting of yourself, you can pav the way for others to be more accepting of you.

The fear of rejection might have started somewhere i your childhood. Perhaps an adult—parent, teacher, etc.– wasn't so accepting of you. Once this happens, as you grov and age, your need for acceptance increases, sometimes s much that it's all you can think of. That fear of never bein accepted for who you are can be very disempowering. Thi might have been what tripped you up. If so, reconcile it an get over it. These people who rejected you in your younge years probably didn't even know they were doing it. And i they did, they might have been in so much pain themselve they couldn't do anything else but. This is where forgivenes and empathy comes into play. Once you can begin to forgiv those who've wronged you, you can let go of these rejectin feelings that cause you so much pain.

While this is all well and good, how do you get ove your fear of being rejected? You just do, that's how. Yo look back and see where it might have started and yo reconcile and you forgive those who rejected you. It's easie said than done, I'll give you that, but if you can do this, yo can set yourself free of these uneasy feeling. You can als open yourself up to better people who won't do you this way.

You can also start putting yourself out there more. Women can't want you if they don't know you exist. If you're not out there getting noticed, then you're not doing yourself any favors.

Most importantly, *don't let rejection stop you.* Keep on going! Yes, you should certainly stop for a moment and recognize your feelings. This will keep you from bottling them up where they can later bubble up and drive you nuts. Just recognize your feelings, whether it's humiliation, embarrassment or being let down. Take a moment and *feel* what you're feeling. Always recognize and then reconcile your emotions. Just don't get hung up on them. And then get back on track. This is one of the most important lessons in this book. It's to get on track and to stay on track until you become the man women want.

One good thing to keep in mind is that if a person really likes themselves, it's harder for them to feel rejected. This is because they're not trying so hard to get acceptance. They're not putting that out there, which can be perceived as being needy or desperate or whatever. They're just trying to make a connection, not trying to be totally accepted and wanted and needed by everyone they meet. Because they like themselves, they know that others will too.

People who like themselves see the situation for what it is. They understand that if they get rejected it just means they weren't compatible with that person or situation. They don't filter all this through the narrow viewpoint of being accepted or rejected.

In the end, just know that if you expect rejection, you will more than likely get rejection. And if you focus so much on it, it can become a reality. So, why not turn it around and instead of expecting rejection, start to expect acceptance?

Just tell yourself, "I'm a good guy and I will be liked by most people I meet. Sure, some of them won't be that compatible with me, but so what? That doesn't make me a bad person or them a bad person. It just means we weren't compatible."

If you begin to believe this, it will happen. This is called having self-acceptance. It's the best way to build confidence. So, get over your fear of rejection, get out there and get to it. Soon enough, if you keep a good attitude and get over your issues with this subject, you will find the acceptance you desire.

What you've got.

Whenever I see someone who is unhappy, alone and frustrated, I wonder if the main reason why is because they're not embracing what they have. By this I mean, don't they like anything about their lives, themselves or the people they know? Why are they so miserable?

If you refuse to embrace your life as it stands right now, it could potentially block newer, better things from appearing. I know this might sound metaphysical or whatever, but I think it's true. This is why I think *it's always a good idea to embrace your life as it is right now.* If you never appreciate what you have, you'll never be happy with anything you've got because it will never be good enough for you.

Take for instance the guy who always gets a new girl. Well, the old one looked pretty good, didn't she? And now he's going on to another one? And, soon enough, there might be another one waiting in the wings. What was wrong with the first girl? Probably absolutely nothing. He probably really liked her, but then another one just appeared from out of nowhere and she wanted to join his party. So he, basically, hopped from one bed to the next.

Now, I don't condone going from one girl to the next like this. Bed-hopping is not my forte. But I have seen it happen. And it always seems to happen to the same kind of guys, too. Who are these guys? They're not *that* great. But they are attracting women into their lives. How? I'd be willing to say that by appreciating the fact they have so many women into them, they open themselves up to having even more women. Mostly, these guys are just having a good time and that's what they've got going for them. So, they're attracting more good times into their lives.

Oddly enough, I've noticed that this kind of stuff never happens to guys who are miserable. It never happens for the ones who are desperate for it to happen. It's always the guys who already have it. Those guys always seem to have all the luck.

Or do they?

Seriously, are they really that lucky? They're just normal guys, right? But why are they having all the luck? Why do women love them? I'd be willing to bet that it has a lot to do with the way they embrace their lives. And who wouldn't embrace a life like that? Cute girls abound! Or, more specifically, cute girls who like to hang with guys like this abound.

The point is, if you don't embrace what you have now, your inability and, perhaps, refusal, to embrace what you have might be keeping the hotties at bay.

Take a moment to digest that.

You might be thinking, "But all I've got is junk!" Wrong attitude, my friend. Sure, what you have might be, in fact, junk. So what? It's what you have! And, most importantly, it's *your* junk. Until you recognize all the good things in your life and start showing gratitude for them, better things might not come along. If you can begin to appreciate what you have—even if you think it's junk—new things can start showing up. This allows more good things to come into your life. The gist is: Stop thinking that all you have isn't good enough. Once you do this and start seeing the good in what you have, you begin to embrace it. If you disown it, new things don't come as easy.

Mostly, you embrace what you have now because it's good. Sure, it might not be as good as so-and-so's, but it *is* good. Your car might not be a sporty coupe, but it runs, right? It does run, right? If so, that's good! You have a car that runs! Good for you! Now appreciate it for all it's worth, even if it has rust holes and the seat's broken.

This is called showing gratitude. And once you're grateful for what you have, you can have even more.

I understand that it can be hard. You might hate your job and, well, who doesn't? You probably can't stand the fact that your good friend, what's-his-name, gets dates all the time and you're alone every Saturday night. Understandable. But does what's-his-name have a mom that bakes delicious cookies? Does what-his-name even know how to change the oil in his car? Probably not. These are your good things. By embracing them, you are saying, "I'm okay. I am not in need." And this opens you up to more good things.

Now these are just examples. I know not everyone has a mom who bakes the most delicious cookies or whatever. The point is to find the good things in your life and appreciate them.

I know that if you have had a bad dating streak, it can be difficult, at best, to see the good in that. But this is just a form of resistance. You are resisting what you have and this just puts up a wall between yourself and what you want.

When this happens, you can get into a funk and I'm not talking about the George Clinton kind of funk. I'm talking about the doldrums. I'm talking about the funk that can last years and weigh you down. When this happens, you begin to wonder why everything is so hard and why you can't get dates and why you can't be happy. Then you start to procrastinate. And, in a way, you just give up. You, then, put yourself into a position where you can't change.

Well, get over it, man! This mindset is exactly what is keeping you from getting better. It's what's keeping you from being the man women want! But by showing appreciation for what you have and for how far you've come, you can get out of the funk! You do not have to wait until the perfect situation comes about to change. You can change right now, today, and start living a better life. If you only see the bad and never look for any good, all you are focusing on is what's wrong with your life. How about this? How about starting to focusing on what's *right*? Do that today. Find one good thing your life and focus on it. Love it. Hug it, figuratively speaking. Or, better yet, hug yourself. mean, if you want to.

If you want to get from A to B, you have to make changes and one of the easiest changes is to start liking—if not loving—what you have, yourself included. Remember you have you. And that's a start. Once you can begin to appreciate yourself, then you can begin to appreciate all you have and then you can start over.

It is never too late to change. Ever! If you could start today, in a year you could have your whole life turned around. But—here's the kicker—*you have to start.* You can' wait forever to turn it around because the future is today. You don't have to wait on something better, either. If you do this, you can get stuck waiting forever. And then your life can start to really suck as you wait on this "something better" to materialize. And all this starts happening because you don't appreciate what you have now.

So start appreciating it. That's all you have to do. This doesn't mean you're settling for less, because you're not settling. Don't get it confused because this fear of settling can and will block better things from coming into your life. All you're doing is showing appreciation. And once you start appreciating what you have, you can appreciate what you *will* have.

Being content does not mean becoming stagnant. It doesn't mean you're going to stay stuck. Just love what you have while you wait for the better things. If you really and truly want to move forward, you just have to appreciate what you have now. This is called not taking what you have for granted. This is showing gratitude.

And that never hurts anything or anyone. So why not try it? Hug it out and then wait for the magic to start happening. What do you have to lose?

For better or for lack.

One reason why you don't embrace everything about yourself is that you might be coming from position of lack. You might be fixated on what you "don't" have and never stop to appreciate what you do. When you are coming from a position of lack, you give up on things, sometimes even before they get started. But if you can remain positive, you open yourself up to things happening.

Once you start coming from a position of lack, lack is pretty much all you're going to have to look forward to. Lack can overtake your life and then you can start to feel like you're not good enough for anything.

And how do you get to this point? To the point of lacking? It's because it's what *you're feeling*. If you think you don't deserve anything in life, you won't be able to get it. Feeling like you deserve better means you *believing* you deserve better. For example, if you've never had a good, steady girlfriend before now, you're probably thinking that won't ever happen. It's like just because you've never *had* one, you will never *have* one.

Get what I'm saying?

I believe that what you think is what you manifest in your life. If you don't think you deserve any better, you won't get it. Ever. I've seen this happen many times. If you think that all the good women are taken, then so they will be. This is sort of like putting blinders on yourself and refusing to take them off. It's like you've got a notion stuck in your head and nothing can change it. This is coming from a position of lack.

If you've ever said, "It's not fair!" then you are definitely feeling this vibe of lack. However, if you actually believe you can and will find someone special—or several someone specials—then you will. This is called adjusting your attitude.

Attitude is everything in dating. It is everything when meeting someone new. It is everything about everything. If you have a bad, lacking attitude, you'll probably never get a better job, place to live or girlfriend. But if you can somehow stay positive and never give up, you will. It's all in your attitude.

The most important thing to remember is that when you come from a position of lack—whenever you say "It's not fair!"—you are basically putting yourself in a position to do without. However, if you can change your attitude, adjust your perspective, then you can change your life. I've seen it happen! All you have to do is recognize that you're doing this and you can and will set yourself up for a better future.

What I want to stress most in this book is that having confidence and good self-esteem is of the utmost importance. When you tackle issues like this and put them to bed, you are overcoming the very obstacles that have kept you out of the game for so long. And, if you're in the game, overcoming these obstacles will give you a head start. You are setting yourself up for better dating and, more importantly, a better life. And isn't that what you really want?

Now what?

Now that you've got it going on, it's time to actually meet some women and put all this into practice. It's time to implement what you've learned. You've taken care of your issues, your self-esteem is growing and you're more confident than ever. You might have even gotten some new clothes and waxed your car. And now it's time to spread your wings and fly. But, er... What's next?

Don't get stuck here, man.

I know that going out there and meeting women might still make you feel a little uneasy. And that's okay. It just means that you have to *feel what you feel*. Feel the feelings as they arise, whether they are fear, hesitation or whatever. And then go through with whatever you were going to do despite those trepidations. You have to push yourself out there. Take a big step and get moving.

And now the question is: But where do you meet women? If you are to put all this into practice, how can you do that? Where are all the women?

Get a clue. You know where all the women are. And you know where to meet them. And where is that? You meet then everywhere! After all, they do share the planet with you, don't they?

Keep in mind that where you meet them, exactly, is irrelevant. You can meet someone in line at the grocery store or at a rodeo or wherever. The important thing to remember is that it's not so much where you meet them than that you do meet them.

Sure, you can make a plan of action to meet women. This list will be comprised of your personal favorite places. Wherever you go, you are bound to run into someone. It's that simple. However, like I said, you can meet women just about anywhere. If you prefer to start dating online, then go for it. If you want to go to clubs, why not?

The point is that it doesn't matter what you do in order to meet women, as long as you do. There's no reason to make a list of all the places you can find women at as women are pretty much everywhere you are. The idea is to get out there and see who's available. And, because you're ready for this and you are putting out a good, positive vibe, women will start looking at you differently. And, maybe, they might come up and start introducing themselves. How cool would that be? It can happen, but you have to get out there in order for it to.

In the end, if you are still unsure of how to meet women, there are people called matchmakers. What these people do is talk with you, make a list of your attributes and then match you up with someone who will be compatible with you. Matchmakers, for some reason, are always overlooked these days. However, they can be a great asset in meeting women. The introduction is pretty much done for you! All you have to do is show up. And when you do show up, put your best foot forward and give this girl a chance. You never know why might happen.

What it all boils down to in the end...

I understand that this is a lot of stuff to consume. I know that I've hit upon a lot of hotspots but that's the point of the book. Just take the advice in increments and use what you can but be willing to be open to the rest. Hey, if it can help you land a hot chick, then all the better. Do whatever it takes to get out there and find yourself a good woman—or women. Your choice.

Always know that you weren't born deficient. What you might have lost over time is the confidence you need in order to date better. You have everything you need; all you have to do is wake it up and use it.

But what it all boils down to in the end is that it's all up to you. It's up to you to use the advice and it's up to your to go out and find women. It's up to you to overcome your issues and get some self-esteem. It's up to you to decide when you are going to take action. I want this book to inspire you to just do that. I want it to help you get over your fear of rejection or whatever else might be holding you back.

Regardless of the games people play in dating or the places they meet, the bottom line is about having relationships. It is not about one set route to the finish line. It is about *you* finding *your* path. It doesn't matter how you get there, it just matters that you do.

Keep in mind that there are plenty of single women in the world. And, yes, they're waiting to meet someone, just like you are. All you have to do is have the desire to meet someone and then see if it happens. Don't ever sell yourself short. If you are really and truly a good guy, it will come out and women will see it. Don't discount yourself and certainly don't discount them. Take the fear out of dating and watch what can happen. Your life could be totally transformed if you can put this into action.

And isn't that what you want? Total transformation? Lots of hot babes? A date on Saturday night? Someone to call when you're feeling lonely? If so, you can make it happen and it starts to happen when you decide it's possible. And it is possible.

Good luck. Have fun. Be safe. And, please, don't use any cheesy pickup lines. Trust me on that one.

Excellent Self-Improvement for Today's Man!

Understanding Women: The Definitive Guide to Meeting, Dating and Dumping, if Necessary by Romy Miller. Taking an in-your-face approach, this book leaves no excuses for you to not only succeed with women but to understand them as well. If this book doesn't do the trick, nothing will.

Chicks: A User's Guide to Dating, Love and Sex by Dag Albright. Packed with insight and information about women, this book will teach even the novice what works with women and how to apply it to everyday life. It will show you hot to get out of the "friend zone" and into the dating zone.

Sex, Your Woman and You: How to Sexually Please Your Woman in the Bedroom and Beyond by Don Asterwood. This book can help you become the lover you always wanted be. It includes tips on how to properly perform cunnilingus, last longer, get more oral sex, overcome premature ejaculation and impotence as well as other things that will help you be able to better sexually please your lover.

Sex Machine: A Man's Guide to What Really Pleases a Woman in Bed by Charlotte Kane. You can give your lover sexual pleasure and massive orgasms. This book explains how. You can become the lover she's always wanted you to be. The good news is that it's not something that's beyond your grasp. The better news is that you can have fun while you learn.

Get Laid Now! The Man's Guide to Picking Up Women and Casual Sex by Tab Tucker. If you're looking for a serious relationship, this is not necessarily the book for you. This book is about enabling you to get down and dirty. It's about helping you achieve that one thing that keeps eluding you in life. If you need some help getting laid, this book can put you on the right track.

Lightning Source UK Ltd.
Milton Keynes UK
27 October 2009

145450UK00001B/63/P